101
POWERFUL
PROMISES

101
POWERFUL
PROMISES

from the
Book of Mormon

WAYNE E. BRICKEY

DESERET BOOK COMPANY
SALT LAKE CITY, UTAH

Library of Congress Cataloging-in-Publication Data

Brickey, Wayne E.
    101 powerful promises from the Book of Mormon / Wayne E. Brickey.
        p.   cm.
    Includes index.
    ISBN 1-59038-487-3 (hardcover : alk. paper)
    1. Book of Mormon—Quotations. 2. Jesus Christ—Promises. I. Title: One hundred and one powerful promises from the Book of Mormon. II. Title: One hundred one powerful promises from the Book of Mormon. III. Title.
    BX8623 2005b
    289.3'22—dc22   2005018983

Printed in the United States of America
Sheridan Books, Inc., Ann Arbor, MI
10 9   8   7   6   5   4   3   2   1

Dedicated to my father,
in whom I saw
the power of promises

CONTENTS

INTRODUCTION: A BOOK OF HOPE 2

1. The Power of Deliverance (1 Nephi 1:20) 4

2. He Prepares a Way (1 Nephi 9:5–6) 6

3. The Prophet of Prophets (1 Nephi 10:4) 8

4. The Timeless Right to Know (1 Nephi 10:17, 19) 10

5. A Holy Birth (1 Nephi 11:8, 13, 19–22) 12

6. A Holy Life (1 Nephi 11:28, 31) 14

7. Judged by Those Who Know (1 Nephi 12:9–10) 16

8. He Will Manifest Himself (1 Nephi 14:1) 18

9. Sure As Iron (1 Nephi 15:23–24) 20

10. According to Their Hearts (1 Nephi 19:14–15) 22

11. Israel to the Rescue (1 Nephi 21:6, 9) 24

12. A Savior for Our Children (1 Nephi 21:24–25) 26

13. Your Afflictions Will Be Gain (2 Nephi 2:1–2) 28

14. A Seer Will Be Raised Up (2 Nephi 3:7) 30

15. Patience for Those Who Don't Know (2 Nephi 9:25–26) . . . 32

16. A Church That Can Heal (2 Nephi 25:20) 34

17. High Interest Investment (2 Nephi 28:30) 36

18. A Book That Keeps Whispering (2 Nephi 29:2) 38

19. The Ancients Will Not Be Forgotten (2 Nephi 29:4–5) . . . 40

20. The Wisdom of Angels (2 Nephi 31:13) 42

21. You Will Know What to Do (2 Nephi 32:5–6) 44

22. Riches for the Right Reasons (Jacob 2:18–19) 46

23. Each Person Is Precious (Jacob 2:21) 48

24. Virtue Is Worth Any Cost (Jacob 2:28) 50

25. A Feast for the Firm (Jacob 3:1–2) 52

26. Growing in Faith (Jacob 4:6) 54

27. Inspiration We Can Understand (Jacob 4:13) 56

28. Saving Those Who Wander (Jacob 5:11, 20) 58

29. Soaring amid Dark Clouds (Jarom 1:4.) 60

30. The Whole Soul (Omni 1:26) 62

31. Using the Very Words (Mosiah 1:3) 64

32. It All Counts (Mosiah 16:10) 66

33. He Notices Immediately (Mosiah 2:22, 24) 68

34. The Debts Are Paid by a God (Mosiah 15:1) 70

35. The Heirs Are the Ones Who Listen (Mosiah 15:11) 72

36. Modest Leaders Have Power (Mosiah 18:26) 74

37. He Takes His Church Seriously (Mosiah 26:21) 76

38. Living Prophets and New Life (Alma 5:10–12) 78

39. Repenting into His Arms (Alma 5:33) 80

40. Promises to the Lamanites (Alma 9:16–17) 82

41. We Will Stand before Him (Alma 11:43) 84

42. Revelation for the Hungry Heart (Alma 12:10) 86

43. Being Led Away from Temptation (Alma 13:27–28) 88

44. He Loves All His Children Everywhere (Alma 26:37) 90

45. Teachers with a Familiar Voice (Alma 29:8) 92

46. A Hard Paved Road (Alma 32:13, 15) 94

47. Growing Your Tree (Alma 32:27–28) 96

48. The Greater Mercy (Alma 33:8) 98

49. Prospering Is a Simple Matter (Alma 36:1) 100

50. The Ongoing Drama of the Book (Alma 37:18) 102

51. The Big Secret About Love (Alma 38:12) 104

52. The Vital "Space" beyond Death (Alma 40:6, 12) 106

53. The Glorious Resurrection (Alma 40:23, 25) 108

54. The True Faith and the True Church (Alma 44:4) 110

55. Disabling the Devil (Alma 48:17) 112

56. The Word and Our Return Home (Helaman 3:29–30) 114

57. The One Safe Spot (Helaman 5:12) 116

58. Hands That Can Seal (Helaman 10:7) 118

59. The Unfettered Offering (3 Nephi 12:23–24) 120

60. The Grown-Up Child of God (3 Nephi 12:44–45) 122

61. Heaven Honors a Quiet Devotion (3 Nephi 13:3–4) ... 124

62. The Generosity of God (3 Nephi 14:7–8) 126

63. A Sign of Real Goodness (3 Nephi 14:16–18) 128

64. Fulfilling the Law Together (3 Nephi 15:5–6, 9) 130

65. His Eye Is Always on Israel (3 Nephi 16:12) 132

66. All May Join the Chosen Family (3 Nephi 16:13) 134

67. A Solemn Testimony to Our Father (3 Nephi 18:7) 136

68. A Special Kind of Prayer (3 Nephi 18:20–21) 138

69. Inviting, Including, and Saving (3 Nephi 18:31–32) ... 140

70. Imitating Heaven (3 Nephi 18:34) 142

71. A Steady People in the Latter Days (3 Nephi 20:21) 144

72. For the Children of the Prophets (3 Nephi 20:25–26) 146

73. A Holy Destiny for the Jews (3 Nephi 20:33–34, 36) ... 148

74. A Marvelous Work to Do (3 Nephi 21:9–10) 150

75. The Dark Things Will Pass Away (3 Nephi 21:19) 152

76. A Greater Savior Than We Think (3 Nephi 22:7–8) ... 154

77. True Servants, Future Kings (3 Nephi 24:17–18) 156

78. Elijah and the Hearts (3 Nephi 25:5–6) 158

79. A Day of Greater Knowledge (3 Nephi 26:9) 160

80. Ensuring a Holy Church (3 Nephi 27:9–10) 162

81. A Book That Persuades the Right People
(Mormon 5:14–15) 164

82. Being Raised to a Great Gathering (Mormon 6:21) 166

83. A World Reserved for the Guiltless (Mormon 7:7) 168

84. A Book of Vital Things (Mormon 7:9–10) 170

85. Treated Like Royalty (Mormon 9:9, 11) 172

86. The One Way of Freedom (Ether 2:12) 174

87. Believe and See (Ether 4:13) 176

88. A Mighty Anchor (Ether 12:4) 178

89. The Power to Change (Ether 12:27) 180

90. The Power to Rejoice (Ether 12:37) 182

91. Power As Well As Priesthood (Moroni 2:2) 184

92. Discernment Equal to the Battle (Moroni 7:12) 186

93. Goodness Leads to More Goodness (Moroni 7:17) 188

94. Charity Lasts (Moroni 7:46–47) 190

95. A Universal Gift (Moroni 7:48) 192

96. Launching a Wonderful and Lawful
Journey (Moroni 8:26) 194

97. Perfect Rest for the Mind (Moroni 9:25) 196

98. The Power of Confirmation (Moroni 10:5) 198

99. Never a Question of Power (Moroni 10:19) 200

100. Becoming Spotless and Perfect (Moroni 10:32) 202

101. Conclusion: An Appointment with
Prophets (Moroni 10:34) 204

NOTES 207

INDEX 217

This book joins the ranks of people and things owing their good fortune to my wife, Joanne. Along with a thousand other services, she rallies the support of our wonderful children, which makes all the difference in a project like this. Gratitude is one of the sweet sensations that come whenever I think of Joanne.

I also thank Cory Maxwell and his associates at Deseret Book. They have become more than colleagues. They are genuine friends.

We are indebted to the original writers behind this book: the prophets who lived in such a way that they could pen the promises. I hope to honor them with more than words.

INTRODUCTION

A BOOK OF HOPE

Which is to show unto the remnant of the House of Israel what great things the Lord hath done for their fathers; and that they may know the covenants of the Lord, that they are not cast off forever—And also to the convincing of the Jew and Gentile that JESUS is the CHRIST, the ETERNAL GOD, manifesting himself unto all nations. (Book of Mormon Title Page, paragraph 2.)

If you have the impression that a lot of promises are made in the Book of Mormon, try counting them sometime. After going at it a while, I realized there were a bit more than a hundred—many hundreds! Thousands! Maybe there should be a big book called *1,001 Powerful Promises*. In the meantime, this book is but a sampler, a jarful from the ocean of tender mercies.

The Book of Mormon is a book of promises, for it is God's book, and he is a God of promises. He makes promises and keeps them. We build our friendship with him by doing the same.

What a range of things Moroni saw! He witnessed the death throes of his once noble nation. He was personally acquainted with the three Nephite disciples who had already outlived the previous few centuries and would live on for many more. He saw angels. He was visited by the resurrected Jesus. He peered into the coming ages as other seers had before him, and he even foresaw his future readers (such as you and me).

Moroni cared for the plates in the last decades of his life. Very likely, he made a habit of reading from them each day, just as you and I do. At some point before laying the record in the earth, he inscribed a last summary. In a few words, he explained the grand purpose of the book: to show its readers "that they are not cast off forever."

The miracles that created the Book of Mormon—the countless sacrifices, the years of giving and working, the unnumbered lives rescued and forfeited, the procession of helpers and sponsors who did their part in the complex drama that brought it before the eyes of mankind—all this was permitted just to show something to us.

That something is that there is hope. No one in the mortal path is "cast off." The book shows it repeatedly for individuals and nations that were nearly out for the count. And even when they really were about to be destroyed, the prophets kept working with them, because there was always hope.

Moroni gives us two solid reasons for this hope. First, because of "the covenants of the Lord"; the assurances the Lord made to the ancients have been re-made to us.

The second reason for hope is that "JESUS is the CHRIST, the ETERNAL GOD." He is the one and only being who can take care of things that go terribly wrong. As the central character in the Book of Mormon, his care for each errant person is featured on nearly every page. He is in the business of "manifesting himself to all nations," including every individual in those nations who thought all hope was gone.

Because of the covenants and the Christ, none is cast off. "How great the covenants of the Lord, and how great his condescensions unto the children of men."[1] And how powerful the promises.

1.

THE POWER OF DELIVERANCE

I, Nephi, will show unto you that the tender mercies of the Lord are over all those whom he hath chosen, because of their faith, to make them mighty even unto the power of deliverance. (1 Nephi 1:20.)

This mighty promise greets us in the opening chapter of the Book of Mormon. Nephi vows, "I will show unto you." On page after page, we see it; the guarantee of tailored and tender deliverance is dependable.

You trust the Lord and so you do his will. That makes you one of his "chosen." His tender attention is upon all your adventures, his mercy distills on you as a great priesthood blessing. You are not excused from difficulty, but you are "mighty" in the midst of it. Then, with perfect timing, "the power of deliverance" moves you on.

Nephi's theme continues in the stories and testimonies of other Book of Mormon prophets. They keep showing us that the promise is real.

One of these stories comes four and a half centuries after Nephi. The people of King Limhi were literally surrounded. Their enemies chose not to murder them, only to live off their labors.[1] Several times the people of Limhi tried to fight their oppressors. But this only resulted in massive fatalities, in swollen ranks of bereaved wives and fatherless children.

After repeated failure, in desperate poverty and depression, there came that moment that always affects time and eternity. Turning to the Lord, "they did humble themselves even to the dust."[2] Slowly, the old promise awakens.

Unexpected forces and puzzle pieces begin to move. For example, a group of strangers—Nephites who just happen to know the way to Zarahemla—show up at their anxious borders. A well-planned escape takes them through a back side of the city. They bid a sudden midnight good-bye to their unhappy home. Everything changes overnight, you might say. With the help of their guides, they migrate to Zarahemla. There they come under the influence of the great King Mosiah, who happens to be a prophet. They receive the ordinances. They become Christ's people. It is another story of deliverance.

Some years after, in the twilight of life, that same Mosiah called to mind the story of Limhi's people and pointed out how the old promise works. "And thus doth the Lord work with his power in all cases among the children of men, extending the arm of mercy towards them that put their trust in him."[3]

"In all cases," trust opens the fortress of God and beckons his mighty ones to our side.

Alma was another who, in old age, knew the promise by heart. "I do know," he said to one of his sons, "that whosoever shall put their trust in God shall be supported in their trials, and their troubles, and their afflictions."[4] To another son, he said it this way: "As much as ye shall put your trust in God even so much ye shall be delivered."[5]

Our sons and daughters ought to learn it from their own parents: The old promise is still true, "in all cases."

2.
HE
PREPARES A
WAY

The Lord hath commanded me to make these plates for a wise purpose in him, which purpose I know not. But the Lord knoweth all things from the beginning; wherefore, he prepareth a way to accomplish all his works among the children of men; for behold, he hath all power unto the fulfilling of all his words. (1 Nephi 9:5–6.)

Before Nephi was ever asked to make those golden plates, he knew the God who always "prepareth a way to accomplish all his works." One of these adventures had to do with another set of plates, the ancient ones made of brass, held deep in the guarded fortress of Laban.

The adventure came one night after Nephi and his brothers had been chased out of town by the powerful and murderous Laban. At that point in history, Jerusalem lay in terraces along the steep southern slope of the holy mount. Nephi stood staring at the walls of the old city. Standing alongside were his beaten-down and bewildered brothers.

It was a daring moment. How prudent was it to steal into this dark place, with its narrow stairways and winding passages, in search of the well-guarded plates? Wasn't the task impossible? Upon this decision hung the destiny of millions, the future of a book of books not yet written, the impact of one dispensation upon an even greater.

If God had not prepared a way to get the plates, the business really was impossible. To have faith at such a moment, you have to believe that God has foreseen all the factors, and that he has already planted special factors you do not see. To Laman and Lemuel, the idea of a God who prepares the way was too ridiculous to consider. To Nephi, it was the most reasonable idea of all. Of course the Great Preparer had gone before them! Even imperfect leaders check things out ahead of time, attend to details, coordinate timing, get things ready. But it was in the service of the Perfect Leader that they stood before these shadowed walls.

He quietly reminded his brothers that the Lord "is mightier than all the earth." So then, "why not mightier than Laban and his fifty, yea, or even than his tens of thousands?" It was a fair question. Like all who trust the Great Preparer, Nephi proposed action: "Let us go up."[1]

Such faith made him equal to his great moments.[2] It makes us equal to ours. History teeters on these moments when key people simply assume that God has prepared a way. Though they don't quite see a path, they know one is there somewhere.[3]

Even before the world itself was made, there were key moments. Even then, the Great Preparer was at work. He groomed situations for people, but he also groomed people for situations.[4] He prepared the Atonement, and also the Atoning One—"the Only Begotten Son, who was prepared."[5]

How interesting that the one who is always preparing a way for us asks that we prepare a way before him.[6] So, as friends, we and he exchange acts of forethought and courtesy. We learn his considerate, preparing way of doing things.

3.
THE PROPHET OF PROPHETS

Six hundred years from the time that my father left Jerusalem, a prophet would the Lord God raise up among the Jews—even a Messiah, or, in other words, a Savior of the world. (1 Nephi 10:4.)

With considerable experience as a corporate financial officer, Harold applied for work at Church headquarters in Salt Lake City. Shortly after being offered a responsible position there, he had this conversation with Russ, his next-door neighbor.

"So, they tell me you'll be working for the Mormon Church."

"Looks like it, Russ."

"And you're going to be rubbing shoulders with some of your General Authorities?"

"That's what they tell me."

"Well," Russ said, lowering his voice, "I hear those leaders of yours aren't so great to work with. One of your members told me that in a place like that, you could lose your 'testimony,' whatever that is."

"I'll tell you what," Harold smiled, "give me a while, and I'll report back."

Often during the next few months, that conversation crossed Harold's mind as he met with various Church leaders in his work. On another Saturday, conversing over the backyard fence, he made his report.

"That testimony you referred to,

Russ, is our certainty about Christ, that he lives and that his Church really is on the earth. My testimony was pretty strong going into my work up there in those offices. If you want, I'll tell you how it's doing now."

Russ leaned against the fence and waited. Harold continued, "I know that mortals aren't supposed to be perfect, but I'm just amazed at these men, Russ. I've worked around great folks before, but I've never seen anything like this in my life. After a meeting the other day, I thought, if you could put their personalities together into one person, you'd really have something. You know, you might have something like I imagine the Savior would be if he were here. It hasn't hurt my testimony to work there, Russ. It has taken my testimony to a new level. I know more about Christ than I ever knew before, just by being around his servants."

It means something wonderful about the prophets that they each manifest a bit of their Master's personality. But it means even more about the Master himself, that it would take all the prophets, together, to give us a vague idea of what he is like. In other words, Christ is the ultimate prophet, the Prophet to the prophets.[1]

This ultimate prophet teaches; he "leadeth thee by the way thou shouldst go," as other prophets do.[2] But he is not like the other prophets. Rather, they are something like him. He is the real teacher, the real leader. Their names inspire; his name saves.[3] They hope to absorb some of his wisdom and might. But for the Prophet of prophets, "the spirit of wisdom . . . and might" comes naturally, for he is the Author of it all.[4]

9

4.
THE TIMELESS RIGHT TO KNOW

I, Nephi, was desirous also that I might see, and hear, and know of these things, by the power of the Holy Ghost, which is the gift of God unto all those who diligently seek him. . . . He that diligently seeketh shall find; and the mysteries of God shall be unfolded unto them, by the power of the Holy Ghost, as well in these times as in times of old, and as well in times of old as in times to come; wherefore, the course of the Lord is one eternal round. (1 Nephi 10:17, 19.)

Evidently, Nephi knew something about the latter days. Even before his sweeping revelations, he realized a time would come when floods of light would cover the earth. People would someday seek God diligently, and the things of God would unfold.

He reasoned—and it was good reasoning—that even a teenager, far removed from the wondrous latter days, could be enlightened by that same power. To him it seemed that the principle should be timeless and even-handed: "He that diligently seeketh shall find."

He sought in the age-old way, the well-rounded way. He lived worthily, he put in the needed study of the word, he pondered with the full effort of his mind, he pled in prayer.[1] *Diligence* pretty well describes it.

And so he *received* in the age-old way. Light came from outside himself and unfolded in his inmost self. He was edified, he was persuaded, he saw, he understood new things. He found that the Lord is consistent from age to age. The clarity and strength and sweetness that would someday bless latter-day people could fill him as well.

Most missionaries have seen people follow this logic of faith. It occurs to some that God would be fair, that he would be just as willing to enlighten one of his children as another, as long as they seek him with equal honesty and effort. Robby was one of these. On hearing the story of Joseph Smith, he said to the missionaries. "That makes sense, but I can find out for sure by asking God, right? If he accepted Joseph Smith's prayer, he should accept mine, right?" The missionaries thought that made perfect sense, and they nodded in agreement.

Robby approached the Lord with that trust, believing that all who honestly seek light are equally entitled to it. After some ten days and nights of prayer and study, living as worthily as he knew how, Robby was answered by the God of Nephi and Joseph Smith. The missionaries listened with gratitude as he pointed out a chair and said, "It happened right there. I had been asking and asking. All I wanted to know was whether it was true. And I got to the point where I wanted to know more than just about anything. I had been reading the Book of Mormon and knelt there before going to bed.

"Even before I started to pray, a really wonderful feeling came through me. It was strong. I knew it was real. It started here"—he pointed to the top of his head—"and filled me and stayed a little while. I knew it was all true. I still know. I always will."

Robby was now an expert on these words: "Every one that thirsteth, come ye to the waters." He knew the thirst. He knew the waters. He knew how to seek them again.[2]

5.
A Holy Birth

I looked and beheld a tree; . . . and the beauty thereof was far beyond, yea, exceeding of all beauty. . . . And I beheld the city of Nazareth; and in the city of Nazareth I beheld a virgin, and she was exceedingly fair. . . . And after she had been carried away in the Spirit for the space of a time the angel spake unto me, saying: Look! And I looked and beheld the virgin again, bearing a child in her arms. And the angel said unto me: Behold the Lamb of God, yea, even the Son of the Eternal Father! Knowest thou the meaning of the tree which thy father saw? And I answered him, saying: Yea, it is the love of God. (1 Nephi 11:8, 13, 19–22.)

Both Lehi and Nephi were shown a beautiful tree. Its fruit was "most desirable above all other fruits; yea, and it is the greatest of all the gifts of God."[1] What sort of tree could bring forth such treasure?

We remember that every life is something like a tree. What we do is the fruit of our lives.[2] The greatest Life ever lived produced something that could be offered to all, that could nourish and immortalize and sanctify all. By his fruits we know him. The Savior is the beautiful tree. His life is the tree of eternal life.

This special life had to be infinite, so that giving it up would be an infinite gift. In only one way could such a life, infinite and yet capable of death, come among us: There must be a holy birth.

One parent must be exalted, almighty, divine. From him—the Father—would come the power of infinite life, and the responsibility to pay the bills for all the children. The other parent must be mortal. From her would come the heritage of an earthbound race. From these two must come one special birth, a Lamb born to die, a Life that could be given for endless populations. There was no other way to provide a Redeemer.

This was no small matter. Oh, what arrangements had to be made, what departures from normal patterns! Only by "the condescension of God," only by his willingness to depart from the classical relationships, only by blending an exalted life with a mortal one could God's very Son be a son of this earth. When the magnitude of it was finally hitting Nephi, the angel asked, "Knowest thou the meaning of the tree?" And Nephi said in awe, "Yea, It is the love of God."[3] This kindly descent of God to our situation, this "condescension" in providing a Lamb for us, is pure love.

No wonder, then, that the meaning of the tree is presented to Nephi, and to us, by the vision of a holy birth. No wonder that this hint is given early in the vision: "After thou hast beheld the tree . . . , thou shalt also behold a man descending out of heaven . . . ; and . . . ye shall bear record that it is the Son of God."[4]

Even more grand than the beautiful tree of a dream is the Life of real history that the tree represents. This is the Life that was promised as a gift to us. It is the one Life that produces eternal life. Grand and beautiful is the Birth that made this Life possible.

In the words of King Benjamin, "The Lord Omnipotent . . . shall come down from heaven among the children of men."[5] He would come down in a wise and necessary drama, a holy display of love.

6.
A HOLY LIFE

I beheld that he went forth
ministering unto the people, in
power and great glory; and the
multitudes were gathered
together to hear him. . . . And I
beheld the Lamb of God going
forth among the children of
men. And I beheld multitudes
of people who were sick, and
who were afflicted with all man-
ner of diseases, and with devils
and unclean spirits. . . . And
they were healed by the power
of the Lamb of God; and the
devils and the unclean spirits
were cast out. (1 Nephi 11:28,
31.)

What sort of life would the Son of Heaven live in the short years between his remarkable birth and death? Remembering who he was before birth—a God of creations and galaxies, and also a God of infinite love—we are not shocked at the promise: He would go forth "ministering unto the people"—blessing them, softening their emergencies, and shoring them up. We are not surprised that he served "in power and great glory."

Of course, this in no way meant parlor tricks. He didn't make dogs talk or pots fly through the air. Fluffy stunts of that kind are the trademarks of those who do not want us to notice how useless and selfish they are.

He came into the world with an appointment to meet the demands of justice. But along the way, the Lamb of God would offer himself in other ways. Every act met more than the immediate, crying need. In dispelling disease and deformity, he proved that he could bless more than the body alone. In dispelling evil spirits, he didn't just quell a present torment but reminded men and devils that he was their God. Everything he did was a teaching and an invitation. He never stopped offering a gift deeper and wider and sweeter than anyone had offered before.

Of course, he was clothed "in a tabernacle of clay."[1] Through his mother, Mary, he was a descendant of earthly folk. So, those who wanted to be dazzled found "no beauty" that would cause them to "desire him" or his offers. They didn't get it, and he didn't force them to get it. In fact, as he approached his grievous appointment with our sins—as he became "a man of sorrows"—some hearers were so heedless, and witnesses so blind, that he "was despised."[2]

Many of his opponents were schooled in the revelations— revelations he had given. They jostled him with smug quotes from the prophets—his prophets. Many bustled out of gatherings in disdain to go ply the Law of Moses, failing to see a thousand hints in the Law designed to bring them to their knees before him. They presumed to teach the one who embodies Truth. They presumed to arrest and imprison the only one who lived perfectly. They rolled their eyes at him who knew their long past, who read the thoughts of their tiny hearts, and who would rule on their future.

If, beyond all this, there is something even more magnificent about his life—and something even more tragic about the hostility of his brothers and sisters—it may be this: He was here doing the will of One even greater.[3] Everything he did between birth and death was a glorifying of the Father.[4] His life fulfilled more than prophecy and more than law. It filled a promise that One would come and show us what the Father is really like.

7.

JUDGED BY THOSE WHO KNOW

Thou rememberest the twelve apostles of the Lamb? Behold they are they who shall judge the twelve tribes of Israel; wherefore, the twelve ministers of thy seed shall be judged of them; for ye are of the house of Israel. And these twelve ministers whom thou beholdest shall judge thy seed. And, behold, they are righteous forever; for because of their faith in the Lamb of God their garments are made white in his blood. (1 Nephi 12:9–10.)

The angel explained this to Nephi as if it were good news. The apostles of the Lamb known to us from the New Testament will oversee the judgment of billions—all the house of Israel. The disciples of the Lamb mentioned in the 3 Nephi account will do this same thing with a portion of the house of Israel—the millions of Lehi's children.

The prophet Mormon also mentions this arrangement.[1] In the judgment, we will be entrusted to true and holy prophets.

Why might this be a welcome promise? Surely the Lord will groom these leaders (and others in the priesthood who may assist). When the great day and last hour rolls around, he will not conduct his perfect work through clumsy judges. They will be far in advance of what manner of men they were in the flesh. They will ably retain many details and perfectly remember who is who.

But just what manner of men were they in the flesh? In their earthly careers, what fitted them for such a key role in my life and your life—the job of being sentinels and keepers, interviewers and decision-makers, at the gates as we pass?

One answer may be that they knew Goodness. For some three years, the Jewish apostles ate and slept around the same campfires with the King of Glory. Day upon day, they walked and talked with the Shepherd of Israel. They beheld Jehovah living a life without any unworthy act or word or desire. This godly Person, though younger than some of them, became a father to them all. They were as his sons. From the closest possible point of view, they saw and knew and touched Righteousness.

Of the twelve Nephite disciples, we could say the same thing. They did not know the mortal Jesus, but they spent unbroken hours and days with the unveiled, glorified Jesus. Such experts will not use the wrong standard.

But there is another reason to trust these judges when we come before them. Along with all else they have seen up close, they know Mercy.

Many a new bishop leaves the stake president's office, after being set apart as a "judge in Israel," wondering what that could mean. Time will teach him. There is more to judgment in Israel than the bare law. Israel has a saving covenant, saving ordinances, the saving blood of Christ.[2] By some of the sweetest experiences a mortal could have, the bishop will see firsthand what the apostles repeatedly saw: Jesus, the true Head of the Church, is not only full of truth but grace as well.[3] It is one of the best parts of being a leader in the holy hands of Christ.[4]

As the angel said to Nephi, even the Twelve are "righteous forever" only because of the power of Christ. They know we are counting on the same miracle.

8.
HE WILL MANIFEST HIMSELF

It shall come to pass, that if the Gentiles shall hearken unto the Lamb of God in that day that he shall manifest himself unto them in word, and also in power, in very deed. (1 Nephi 14:1.)

The Lamb of God can manifest himself to us "in very deed"—directly, visibly, in person. But if this is to be a joyous experience, he must first be manifest "in word, and also in power." Otherwise, to meet him abruptly, unprepared, unprotected, unworthy—unacquainted with his word and his power—is to meet him but briefly, and with piercing grief.

We remember Laman and Lemuel, who always seemed to draw a blank when great things were at hand, "because they knew not the dealings of that God who had created them."[1] Following a living God is sometimes a treat and other times a test. But it is always acceptable to those who are immersed in his word and who permit themselves to feel and trust his power.

We can see this lesson in the way temples are designed.

On the south slope of the Temple Mount in Jerusalem, Mike—a studious 14-year-old—asked the guide, "Why are these steps different sizes? The people who built them weren't just making mistakes, were they?"

The guide sighed with relief. "I wondered when someone would ask.

You're very observant." With a sweep of his arm, the guide pointed at the wide and magnificent old stairs. "Look at this. They made the steps of various sizes to keep people from hurrying as they came to the House of the Lord. In fact, sometimes people would stop and sing a hymn or study a verse of scripture at certain points along the way, so that when they got in there, they were ready."

In later years, Mike commented, "That idea means a lot to me now in my temple attendance. I notice that there are steps, and that we move toward the holiest rooms by stopping in other rooms, reviewing and committing ourselves along the way. You can't hurry toward the Lord."

Nephi promised that those who hearken unto the Lamb of God will find him manifest. This comes by small degrees, privately—in word at first, then in power. That is the way he prefers. That way guarantees a permanent connection with him.

When at last he is manifest to us "in very deed," it can be the most wondrous experience we have ever had, a time when he can add instruction and complete the polish and finishing touches to our souls.[2] Then to us, as Isaiah described it, "shall the Son of Righteousness arise with healing in his wings."[3]

Ultimately, "he will make himself manifest unto all."[4] But we are not waiting until the curtain is taken away, when the test is over and the Master stands revealed to his friends and foes alike. We are trying to become his friends in season—now.

The Messiah is not in hiding while the time ripens for his coming. His people have his words and counsel, and they know the modest movements of his power. They are drawing close, and he is making himself manifest.[5]

9.
SURE AS IRON

They said unto me: What meaneth the rod of iron which our father saw, that led to the tree? And I said unto them that it was the word of God; and whoso would hearken unto the word of God, and would hold fast unto it, they would never perish; neither could the temptations and the fiery darts of the adversary overpower them unto blindness, to lead them away to destruction. (1 Nephi 15:23–24.)

A good teaching moment came up one day when someone asked Nephi about the iron rod. If Father's dream was so brilliant and inspired, why was that in there? A person of Nephi's time would be shocked at the extravagance of a handrail streaking through the wastes and valleys of the vast desert. Who would build such a thing?

But this we should know: If a desert separated you from God, he would go to the expense to install such a thing. He built the desert, you might say, to see whether you really wanted to go home. He built a handrail straight across the land to get you there.

For Lehi's clan, it was not really made of iron but of brass. At the time Nephi's brothers asked about the rod, the brass plates had been in camp for months.[1] They sat in one of the tents, waiting to be read and pondered, waiting to guide and build anyone who would take the time.

There was plenty of need for guiding and building people. This group had a normal array of personalities—and perhaps some

20

stronger than normal. Things sometimes got out of hand. In the face of human temptations—the downward pull to be lazy or disloyal or angry, for example—some family members succumbed now and then, and great setbacks followed. That sort of thing isn't necessary, because a source of healing sat in a nearby tent.

The desert was designed to be uncrossable without a handrail. But the handrail—straight and strong—is installed.

The straight rod has kept countless people true to their course in confusing times. The words speak little about medicine. But the spring of light somehow inspired a single mother to find a solution to her son's illness. After reading the scriptures awhile, a missionary couple was guided in their search for a place to live in an unfamiliar land. An hour in the standard works each day somehow enabled an overworked accountant to meet his deadlines during tax season. If we hold to it, the rod will lead us straight ahead.

The strong rod steadies even the shakiest travelers, so that their strides are safe and certain. For example, to those maimed by crystal meth addiction, recovery efforts can be futile until a daily dose from the words of life is added. The scriptures give power to any effort to rise above weakness. God has put a wonderful iron power in his words.

All that straightness and strength, and putting the rail within our reach, has been quite an expense. But to him whose words are presented there, it was worth the trouble. Now we must use our reach. Now we must consider it worth the trouble to hold to it all the way home.[2]

10.
ACCORDING TO THEIR HEARTS

Because they turn their hearts aside, saith the prophet, and have despised the Holy One of Israel, they shall wander. . . . Nevertheless, when that day cometh, saith the prophet, that they no more turn aside their hearts against the Holy One of Israel, then will he remember the covenants which he made to their fathers. (1 Nephi 19:14–15.)

What Nephi said of the Jews is true of all peoples. When their hearts turn from the Holy One, they are left very much alone. When their hearts turn back to him, the old blessings return. Everything depends on where the heart—the eye of desire—is looking.

We sometimes hear of being "in tune," a reminder that we need to get ourselves in harmony with the willing signals that are always there. In the case of heavenly messages, there is no dial to turn. Tuning a heart is a matter of turning it.

How is a heart turned to the Lord? In practical ways. Alma said the "affections of thy heart" are determined by "all thy doings," goings, and thoughts.[1]

A young father illustrated it in this way: "My daughter, Emma, loves pink. This love seems to permeate her existence. It influences her decisions, and especially the clothes she picks out. This struck me one Saturday after a load of Emma's laundry had finished drying. I cleaned out the lint screen in the dryer, and the lint was pink. 'Wait a minute,' I thought, 'isn't lint supposed to be gray?' I checked the laundry trash can, and sure enough, lots of little gray wads of lint in there. Except for Emma's. Her lint was pink. I would like the gospel to permeate my life like that."

A coach was asked what it meant for an athlete to have "heart." He answered, "To me it means they give everything. They give it their all, even in practice . . . especially in practice! That's where most athletes decide how much they're going to give. They aren't just training their bodies in practice. They're training their loyalty, their determination."

Then the question, "So it isn't so much about talk, about strong words?"

"It isn't anything about words. After you've been coaching a while, you stop paying attention to all the big talk. You notice what people actually do."

Turning our hearts to God is specific. He might say to us, "So you want to turn to me? Good. Can you start by praying to me every day and night? I know you aren't used to it, that it may seem embarrassing, or that you think it is a bit hypocritical. But I'm asking you to do it anyway, every day, for the rest of your life. That will be a show of heart."

Or he might say, "If you want to turn to me, I have just the thing. I have a Church. It holds meetings. I would like you to be at these meetings every Sabbath for the rest of your life, as long as you have the slightest strength to show up. Of course, you'll have to plan out your time and your sleep and your transportation and even your health and clothing and perhaps some of your money to do this. That's why I will take it personally, as a token from your heart."

11.
ISRAEL TO THE RESCUE

It is a light thing that thou shouldst be my servant to raise up the tribes of Jacob, and to restore the preserved of Israel. I will also give thee for a light to the Gentiles, that thou mayest be my salvation unto the ends of the earth. . . . That thou mayest say to the prisoners: Go forth; to them that sit in darkness: Show yourselves. (1 Nephi 21:6, 9.)

I srael's mission is both vast and joyous. The size of the work—to rescue so many—need not overwhelm us. The Lord says "it is a light thing." He can handle it. As for the joy, what could be better than liberating those who "sit in darkness"? We are glad to have such good work, and to have so much of it.

Israel is more than a special lineage. The special greatness comes with the covenant. When the covenant is kept, it produces greater-than-normal people, with special stories and elite desires.[1]

Each branch of Adam's family will be beckoned in, invited to liken themselves to Israel. And not only liken, but enlist—become equal citizens.[2] Their blessings are both temporal and spiritual—choice lands and choice knowledge.[3] Most choice of all is to "know their Redeemer, who is Jesus Christ, the Son of God."[4] In a world that has forgotten him, former prisoners know the God of Israel as their own God.

A servant's desire entered the heart of Odindu when he was yet a boy. In those days, the people of his village were still getting their water from a river several miles away. It was a laborious, time-consuming walk. And in the time of Nigeria's civil war, it was dangerous. As the oldest boy in his family, Odindu went for the water almost every day. Often, when the bullies were looking for trouble along the river, he would lay down in a familiar hideout, his large covered bucket next to him in the grass, and wait for them to move on. As he waited, he would pray, "Father in Heaven, it is a great shame that my people live this way. Help me to survive, and let me help them someday."

Odindu did survive. He became one of those heroes who brought the war to an end. He married a girl of like mind. They became educated and devoted themselves to lifting their people. They moved away for a time, to equip themselves for greater service. Odindu gained a doctor's degree but also something else of greater value to his people. He and his wife discovered and embraced the restored gospel. Now they were allied with the powers of heaven, enlisted in the eternal nation known as Israel.

Like an Israelite named Mosiah arriving in Zarahemla, like an Israelite named Ammon approaching the lands of King Lamoni, like 2,000 stripling Israelites going off to defend the Nephites, Odindu was equipped to help.[5]

Thanks to a new couple in Israel, clothed in light, the villagers no longer walk those miles to get their water. And now other Waters are also in reach. The God of Israel honored a servant's prayer in ways that a noble boy, crouched on a riverbank, could not have imagined.

In a hundred nations and a million stories, the mission—vast and joyous—continues.

12.
A Savior for Our Children

Shall the prey be taken from the mighty, or the lawful captives delivered? But thus saith the Lord, even the captives of the mighty shall be taken away, and the prey of the terrible shall be delivered; for I will contend with him that contendeth with thee, and I will save thy children. (1 Nephi 21:24–25.)

Why should lawful captives be delivered? Don't they deserve their bondage if it is "lawful"? Who would ask for such a suspending of justice? A mother or father, no doubt. "Is there no hope, no second chance for my child—weak and brash as he was? Can he not be freed from the slaver's hand?" A deaf, inflexible universe gives no answer. But from the One called Savior we hear, "I will save thy children."[1]

The promise means a lot to the parent of righteous children. It means even more to the parent who mourns over a captive child, as Nephi mourned over his seed, "O the pain, and the anguish of my soul. . . . It well nigh consumeth me."[2]

Jacob, younger brother to Nephi, uttered the promise in these words. "Our children shall be restored."[3] Jacob later explained how the wayward, "having rejected the sure foundation, can ever build upon it." The famous story of the olive trees helps Jacob to "unfold this mystery."[4] In simple terms, the Lord of the vineyard takes two measures to save his wild and fruitless trees: pruning and nourishing.[5]

By pruning, people are humbled, reduced and scattered. Sometimes we can only look on as the untiring Pruner works slowly to save those we love. In such times, until their own day of righteousness, what our wayward ones need most is our righteousness.

As the untiring Nourisher, he writes his word to the minds of our children and whispers it into their hearts.[6] No matter how long and far they wander, he "is still calling after" them.[7] We trust the untiring Christ to remember "all them who have been broken off."[8] Faith gives permission to the miracle.

From the return of Alma the Younger, we know that the miracle of return also needs the prayers of friends and family.[9] And so we keep praying for our children and the children of others.[10]

Some seventy years after Alma's return, two of his great-grandsons fell into the hands of hostile people while serving a mission. Walls trembled, fire surrounded, the voice of Deity whispered, souls were converted. And a certain Aminadab, formerly a dissenter from the Church, was crucial to the event. This was the day of his return.[11] We suppose there were loved ones somewhere praying for Aminadab. He was reclaimed with a mighty hand.

"All thy children shall be taught of the Lord; and great shall be the peace of thy children."[12] Thus stated Jesus, quoting from his prophet Isaiah.

No wonder the Lord commands, "Lift up your heads forever, because of the blessings which the Lord God shall bestow upon your children."[13] It is our pleasure to keep that commandment.

13.
YOUR AFFLICTIONS WILL BE GAIN

Thou hast suffered afflictions and much sorrow. . . . Nevertheless, . . . thou knowest the greatness of God; and he shall consecrate thine afflictions for thy gain. (2 Nephi 2:1–2.)

J acob had suffered "afflictions and much sorrow"—we are not told what kind—because of the extreme "rudeness" of Laman and Lemuel.[1] But, Lehi could say, "Thy soul shall be blessed." God oversees affliction with a particular compassion. At the right time, struggle translates to strength, loss converts to gain.[2] Jacob would someday be cared for by Christ, "even as they unto whom he shall minister in the flesh."[3] All who are similar to Jacob can look forward to this blessing.

Mortal life isn't some nasty reality that won't go away. It doesn't perplex God. Mortality is not a normal part of the large, smooth-running, pleasant universe he governs. There would be no such place if our personal growth did not call out for a short, intense stretch of bumpy road. It is for our schooling that we have temporary handicaps in us and baffling circumstances around us.[4] The school is just right.

God designed this peculiar island of sorrows, purposely different from the vast and peaceful realms that surround it. Since he made every bit of this world from scratch, from the blueprint up, he can discontinue it and make it a thing of the past when he wants.

That's just what He is going to do with this lesser world as soon as it fills its purpose. He won't take that action a minute too soon, but when the last student has emerged, the place must go.

We have only a glimpse of the trauma that came to Alma and his companion Amulek. They were imprisoned, starved, and beaten. Worse by far was watching as their converts and friends were burned to death.[5] Some of Amulek's family, so blessed at one point, were likely tortured and destroyed in that holocaust.[6] By the time Alma was able to get Amulek to a new home and "administer unto him in his tribulations," the toll must have been devastating.[7]

Amulek's afflictions were too great for others to quite understand. But he was also entitled to a joy so complete and private that others could understand it only by experiencing it.[8] Our afflictions, and our gains, are private—between us and the Lord.

Disasters—private or widespread—shouldn't be seen as a spanking intended for sinister children. They come upon even the most noble and savvy immigrants from heaven. Despite their long training in higher circles, they come here for intense teaching moments. They need lessons given in unforgettable ways.

The Creator watches and waits for our graduation. Arrangements have been made for our homecoming celebration; the mansion is being built even now.[9] The "gains" are being prepared, and so are we.

14.
A Seer Will Be Raised Up

Yea, Joseph truly said: Thus saith the Lord unto me: A choice seer will I raise up out of the fruit of thy loins; and he shall be esteemed highly among the fruit of thy loins. And unto him will I give commandment that he shall do a work for the fruit of thy loins, his brethren, which shall be of great worth unto them. (2 Nephi 3:7.)

The Hebrew name *Joseph* combines more than one meaning: adding on and taking away.[1] Joseph Smith's work of gathering and restoring called for both. Stamp collectors don't keep every stamp they find. They cull and discard what has no value. To restore an old castle, you would keep the useful, eliminate the useless, and add what is missing. Joseph did all this.

To do it, he needed super powers of sight. Seers are good at seeing. "Things shall be made known by them which otherwise could not be known."[2]

That is true not only of earthly things but also of heavenly things. And not only heavenly things but also Heavenly Beings. Joseph the Seer acted as our eyes.

We admit that our sight is poor whenever we wear glasses, or when we trust what scientists see through microscope or telescope, or when we believe the results of an X-ray. But those puny devices don't unveil what the seers know of the past, the future, the big picture, the great plan, and "the meaning of all things."[3]

So it is stunning that we would

actually have a seer among us. In addition, we were promised he would be "choice"—someone we would really like. In premortal times, when we knew so much and all the lights were on, this noble one was an easy choice. But in a dimly lit world, some find it difficult to choose him anew.

From the Lord's words to an ancient Joseph, we have good reasons to choose our latter-day Joseph. For example, he would not only be "great," but he would also grow to greatness "out of weakness."[4] His greatness would not be showy. It would be expressed in lots of work, and in making a dramatic, eternal difference.[5] And no one would be able to overturn his work.[6]

It would not only be the seer himself that would be great; his very words would go with force into people's souls.[7] Though simple, the words would be deep and "strong."[8] It would be as if our most righteous and caring ancestors were crying out to us.[9] Those words would be just right—spiritually "expedient"—for anyone, anywhere, anytime.[10]

And those who hearkened to the strong Seer would become strong themselves.[11] The words would settle every important question, bring accord where there was dispute, instill peace where there was turmoil.[12]

The work of the choice seer isn't yet finished. The old castle hasn't been entirely restored, and all its heirs are not yet home. We, and billions unborn, will need to keep choosing this Seer and his companion seers for quite a long time.

15.

PATIENCE FOR THOSE WHO DON'T KNOW

Where there is no law given there is no punishment; and where there is no punishment there is no condemnation; and where there is no condemnation the mercies of the Holy One of Israel have claim upon them, because of the atonement. . . . For the atonement satisfieth the demands of his justice upon all those who have not the law given to them. (2 Nephi 9:25–26.)

This is a sweeping and basic promise: Christ will cover with mercy all those who are without law—who don't understand what God expects of them. The principle gives rise to many doctrines. And it applies to many of our relationships.

Several centuries after Jacob announced the principle, King Benjamin described how it applies to children: "Little children . . . are blessed; for . . . the blood of Christ atoneth for their sins."[1] Of course. Little children "have not the law given to them." Every wise parent in King Benjamin's audience must have loved those words.

Some five centuries later, Mormon did what Benjamin had done. He pointed out how the sweet and sweeping promise applies to children: "Little children are whole, for they are not capable of committing sin."[2]

But the larger principle—which applies so absolutely to children— applies in part to some big people too. If a person is missing major pieces of the law, Christ covers them, and they are not expected to live those parts. If there is a tendency to judge those whom Christ has clothed in mercy,

Mormon might say, "Wo be unto them that shall pervert the ways of the Lord after this manner."[3] And Alma might add, "Let the justice of God, and his mercy, and his long-suffering have full sway in your heart."[4]

If we try to look into hearts, we find many who don't want to be lost. Perhaps there is some fault in early youth when the light was brighter, the voice of right more crisp.[5] But if all that has dimmed—if they walk in confusing shadows—how shall we feel toward them? Would we condemn the lost? Might not many of them correct their course if they could see and hear again?

To suppose that disoriented people intend to be bad is a pretty harsh view of human folly. Mormon might call this harshness "awful wickedness, " for it denies the "pure mercies of God unto them."[6] He would remind us that God is not "partial"—nicer to some just because they were raised with more light and knowledge.[7]

Benjamin said that what we all need is "the knowledge of a Savior."[8] Some do not consider themselves worth saving until this assurance rises like the morning sun in their understanding. Repentance is inspired, not merely by guilt but also by the hope of being forgiven, the hope that weaknesses can be healed and guilt swept away.

If adults without a sunrise are somewhat accountable, they are certainly not counted out.[9]

"O how marvelous are the works of the Lord, and how long doth he suffer with his people."[10] His suffering isn't mere silence. When the time is right, he sends understanding. Until then, mercy.

16.
A Church That Can Heal

As the Lord God . . . gave unto Moses power that he should heal the nations . . . if they would cast their eyes unto the serpent which he did raise up before them, . . . there is none other name given under heaven save it be this Jesus Christ, of which I have spoken, whereby man can be saved. (2 Nephi 25:20.)

About six centuries before Nephi's time, his ancestors lived in a harsh, wide wilderness under the leadership of Moses. Their "church," as we might call it now, was made up of the twelve nations known as Israel. There came a crisis when many of those people were bitten by "fiery flying serpents." Just about anyone not lying in agony at the point of death was looking on in horror and despair, unable to help dying loved ones.

What did the great prophet do about the situation? In the saving name of the Messiah, he set up a pole on which was fixed the brass figure of a serpent. It was a reminder. It represented the One who would someday take their place, who would receive the venom for all mankind. In that wilderness church, Moses asked that they merely turn and look upon the sacred token of Christ. Each who would do this, he promised, would be healed.[1]

The promise continued to Nephi's time and is still in force. The brass figure was a temporary means of trusting in Christ. But healing is still offered to those with that trust—who trust his name, his Church, and the other tokens he has given.

In 34 A.D., the Nephites were reeling from calamity. Thunderous forces of nature had reduced their world to eerie rubble. But through the heavy dust they heard the healing Christ: "Will ye not now return unto me, and repent of your sins, and be converted, that I may heal you?"[2] Turning to him and his Church, they were made whole.

Again in our day, we have a Church that can heal, for the Head of this Church is that same Healer.

Once, not many years ago, there were two men of separate lands—nations often in vicious war with each other. One man had witnessed an attack in which numerous loved ones were massacred. The other man was a commanding officer in the attacking forces.

The years brought each man, under separate circumstances, into contact with a particular Latter-day Saint couple. Each man embraced the gospel. Each grew spiritually, against all sorts of resistance, in his own culture. Then came an evening to be remembered, when both men happened to be visiting the United States at the same time. Inside the home of that same Latter-day Saint couple, one man peered intently out the entry window as he waited. The other man at last drove up to the house, sat in the car for what seemed a long time, and then walked slowly to the door.

A pause. A quiet knock. A door opens, and two former enemies—now elders of Israel—look upon each other in a new Light. Witnessed by a few close friends, and under the eyes of the Healer, the men step forward and embrace. In the saving name of Christ, another healing—like that which will at last "heal the nations."

17.
HIGH
INTEREST
INVESTMENT

I will give unto the children of men line upon line, precept upon precept, here a little and there a little; and blessed are those who hearken unto my precepts, and lend an ear unto my counsel, for they shall learn wisdom; for unto him that receiveth I will give more. (2 Nephi 28:30.)

To "him that receiveth" light, more is promised. When a tree receives light through its leaves, everything gets larger and stronger, including the leaves. Larger leaves welcome even more light, and the growth goes on at new levels.

Amulek once pled with an audience to "contend no more against the Holy Ghost, but that ye receive it"— to welcome that influence, to take it in, even to pull it in.[1] The promise is as old as light itself. We are reminded of it each time someone is confirmed a member of the Church.[2]

Where shall we find evidence of this promise? In every faithful member of the Church!

Yes, there are more notable cases, like Roksana, the 14-year-old girl who teaches the Gospel Doctrine class in her little branch. She emerged from her first reading of the Book of Mormon aglow with testimony. She seems to abound in new understanding every time she ponders the scriptures.

But in private hearts there are evidences on every row of every sacrament meeting. For every Roksana, there are many Vasilis. Also new in the Church,

Vasili is a more typical member of Roksana's branch. He did not glow quite so much, you might say, until several months of study with the missionaries. They and his wife despaired of his ever gaining a testimony. But steadily, like the adding of one thin line of thread after another to a giant, empty loom, he grew in light and certainty. After baptism, his growth is ever steady. He is teaching the gospel now, at home mostly. The simplicity and clarity of his teaching is the result of a deep, permanent understanding.

We remember the story of the sons of Mosiah, whose leaves got so large that they went from young men full of ignorance and distortion to being "men of a sound understanding." But we should remember that this expansion took fourteen years, and that "they had searched the scriptures diligently, that they might know the word of God."[3] They were interested day and night, receptive day and night. The old law is that if you are interested and receptive, you will receive more and more light.

It was by that same law that thousands of others, who heard the words of the sons of Mosiah, also grew from precept to precept as these missionaries did. The converts are to us unnamed and yet well known to the heavens, where they now dwell in light. Even in this life, starting in "darkness and destruction," they became "encircled about with the matchless bounty" of light and love.[4]

How does this growth take place? Larger and larger leaves. Being receptive. Receiving, welcoming. The growth is happening in every sacrament meeting, in every home and every heart where there is a high rate of interest.

18.
A BOOK THAT KEEPS WHISPERING

The words of your seed should proceed forth out of my mouth . . . and my words shall hiss forth unto the ends of the earth, for a standard unto my people, which are of the house of Israel. (2 Nephi 29:2.)

Down in the canyons and across the ranges of cattle country just about anywhere can be heard the sharp "hiss" of cowboys, directing the traffic of their herds. The sustained "s" sound pierces the distance between man and animal, the high frequency clearly distinguished from other noises.

The words of the Lord are tuned to the ears of his sheep. Their ears were created to hear the words. He has solemnly promised that the words engraved by Nephite prophets would "hiss forth" to all the pastures and hillsides of the earth, and that every willing ear would come alive at the special sound.

The book will be a common love among honest hearts. It will help the Lord select from the nations those who are interested in the right things for the right reasons.[1] Its voice, so different from voices in the writing of men, is just right for this purpose. It is his voice.

And the Spirit of the Book of Mormon is "a standard" for his people. By the spirit we feel from it, we may judge other claims to spirituality. What does not measure up to the whispering of that book is not worthy of our loyalty.

In the highlands of Guatemala, our group of Latter-day Saints boarded a boat and slowly crossed Lake Atitlán, trying to memorize the shoreline, trying to picture ancient scenes. But we soon discovered that on board with us was a tiny young Cakchiquel woman, there to offer her blankets and jewelry for sale. Her people had been living in this place since Book of Mormon times. That we knew. Somehow, the thought of this drew our attention from the far-off scene to the daughter of the past sitting before us.

Out of someone's bag came a Book of Mormon; several spoke to her about old prophets and noble families—not our prophets and families but Maria's, no doubt. The skipper stopped at mid-lake and shut off the big diesel engine. In the quiet, someone rehearsed a story from the book. Gentle testimonies were born. Maria listened, wide-eyed, motionless, simple in her poverty, rich with innocence, immediate in her belief.

Maria has since embraced the Church, and it has embraced her. But there was a moment on the lake that lives on. It was when lesser things were upstaged by the whisper of absolute certainty. Like the hiss of fire or the hiss of a two-edged sword, the moment burned in and sank deep, for us and for Maria.

The Book of Mormon will keep whispering. It will keep stopping boats and finding the honest Marias. It will pierce and burn into the inner parts of mankind until all have been reached. It will hiss across boundaries and shake souls at the core, until every mind has decided. It will go "unto the ends of the earth."

19.
THE ANCIENTS WILL NOT BE FORGOTTEN

What thank they the Jews [and the Lamanites] . . . ? Do they remember the travails, and the labors, and the pains of the Jews [and the Lamanites], and their diligence unto me . . . ? I the Lord have not forgotten my people. (2 Nephi 29:4–5.)

The Lord has promised to remember the unselfishness of faithful parents, whether it be their prayers or their travails, whether they be Jewish faithful or Nephite, whether faithful little girls or faithful old men.[1]

At a funeral for a man who had lived to nearly 90, one of the speakers said something most of us had not thought of before. He reviewed some of the historic and quaint things of the "old days" when Lee was a child. "That was the world around Lee. But the world inside him was a lot like the world inside most little boys, no matter when they live. He liked to play outside as long as he could on a warm evening. He liked watermelon, and ice cream if he could get it. He probably liked to tease a girl every now and then.

"But when Lee grew up, and became an 80-year-old and then an almost 90-year-old," the speaker continued, "he had changed on the inside even more than the world changed over the years. That's our Father's plan, you know. We would live in this world a while and change. What I mean is that the grown up and old Lee hardly ever thought about himself." The speaker paused and let Lee's friends remember that this was true.

"Now, who do you think he thought about the most? He thought about his wife of course, but also his children, and his grandchildren. I was with him a while back when he offered a prayer. He prayed for his children. Life had changed Lee from a single little boy into a real father. He had become a patriarch in his heart."

Eight-year-old Sarah was always a bright and spiritual little girl. But even her parents were not prepared for the announcement she made one morning before family prayer. "I had a dream about my children."

The father was just picking up the two-year-old to prevent a crafty escape but set him back down and looked at Sarah. "Children you're going to have someday?" he asked.

"I guess so. I had a husband in the dream, and we had four children."

The mother sat down next to Sarah. "So go on. What about these children of yours?"

"Well, in the dream I could sort of tell there was a lot of noise and bad outside our house, like way out in the world." Sarah looked at the floor, thinking back as if the dream were a real experience. She looked up at her mother. "Could we pray for my children today?"

Most of us take a little longer than Sarah, or even Lee, to start praying for generations unborn. But those feelings—like the feelings of the ancient Saints—are heaven-sent. They finally come. We come to feel that our grandchildren of the distant future are just as real as our living family. We come to love them and pray for them. The Lord doesn't forget those prayers.

20.
THE WISDOM OF ANGELS

If ye shall follow the Son, with full purpose of heart, acting no hypocrisy and no deception before God, but with real intent, repenting of your sins, witnessing unto the Father that ye are willing to take upon you the name of Christ, by baptism— yea, by following your Lord and your Savior down into the water, according to his word, behold, then shall ye receive the Holy Ghost; yea, then cometh the baptism of fire and of the Holy Ghost; and then can ye speak with the tongue of angels, and shout praises unto the Holy One of Israel. (2 Nephi 31:13.)

The great work of the Son was to make an offering only he could make. But there was another task for him alone: to demonstrate a perfect life. He showed us the essentials. Nephi could list those essentials, for he saw the perfect life in vision.[1]

The first essential is easy for mortals to forget, so Nephi emphasized it: "full purpose of heart." Without this, we take the marked path without really choosing it, only because it happened to be in front of us. Or, because our friends happen to be traveling there. But sooner or later we will need to follow Jesus out of pure trust and love for him.

The gospel isn't just routines. It is called "the gospel of Jesus Christ" because it is really about him. Why do we follow it? For a personal reason: We follow it to follow him.

But "full purpose" withers under hypocrisy. Only pretending to care is a "deception before God" that doesn't fool God. It only fools us, leaving the false impression that "all is well."[2] If the motive is wrong, nothing is well.

Another term for "full purpose of

heart" is *faith*. As the Son followed his Father in faith, so we follow the Son. We trust his steps, so we trace his steps. The first essential is faith.

The second essential, "real intent," is the spine of repentance. Of course, Jesus needed no repentance. But in his real intent—his resolve to do the Father's will—he gave us the key to his sinlessness, and the key to our repentance from sin.

And where does his path take us next? Into the water. That is where he "witnesseth unto the Father that he would be obedient unto him."[3] It is where we too make a binding, public promise. The weekly sacrament keeps this third essential fresh and new.

After Jesus emerged from the waters of promise, "the Holy Ghost descended upon him."[4] This the fourth essential, to receive a divine Companion.

After Nephi lists these four essential principles, he tells of two blessings that follow. One of these is a baptism in fire. Under the supervision of the Holy Ghost, we will be immersed in cleansing light, soaked in new life.

Another promised blessing is "the tongue of angels"—not just sacred ways of expressing things but also sacred things to express. What wise and sacred things, above all, do the angels feel to speak? Nephi's answer: "Praises unto the Holy One of Israel."[5] What is in the heart of the Holy Ghost? "Hosanna to the Lord, the most high God."[6] What were the wise beings of heaven doing when Alma saw them? "Praising their God." After following the Son faithfully, we will say, with Alma, "My soul did long to be there."[7]

21.
YOU WILL KNOW WHAT TO DO

If ye will enter in by the way, and receive the Holy Ghost, it will show unto you all things what ye should do. Behold, this is the doctrine of Christ.
(2 Nephi 32:5–6.)

The wise hosts of higher worlds honor the Lord. By the "tongue of angels," we join in.[1] And our bond with the Holy Ghost and with angels goes beyond this. The "tongue of angels" can make us wise in our daily walk.[2]

As leaders and teachers speak week by week, or when sacred writings are open before us day by day, Christ is free to fit the words to us. Hour by hour, he has a direct channel to the open heart. It can be a feast for the inner ear, we might say.

"Feast upon the words of Christ; for behold, the words of Christ will tell you all things what ye should do."[3]

Our privilege is not only to hear but also to do. If we wait only for ideas that require no action, we may miss most of the messages. Even when things don't entirely make sense or when we don't feel very well or very happy, the Guide will give the revelation needed most of all—he "will tell you all things what ye should do."

Fourteen-year-old Jerry was a little discouraged. Like a few other Eagle projects in the history of the world, his had been dragging on for months. Some 600 small wooden blocks, destined to go into toy bags for needy children, had been individually cut, sanded smooth, and primed. They were now being painted various colors.

"How many coats is this going to take, anyway?" he wondered. The gray primer still showed under two coats of yellow paint. Then he looked at the blocks while squinting his eyes. Sure enough, if you looked in a blurry sort of way, the gray didn't show at all. And if you turned off the lights, and blocked the garage window with a big box, the blocks looked perfect.

But Jerry was a good boy, and he knew he was kidding himself. He knew there was a voice inside for times like this. So he braced himself a little and checked for that voice.

He could imagine a child playing in the sand of some far-off land. The child's hands, a beautiful dark bronze in color, were caressing some glossy, bright yellow blocks.

Jerry picked up one of the blocks and ran a finger over the surface. Smooth here but still a little rough there. Glossy and solid yellow in spots but mostly dull and imperfect. An impression came to Jerry's mind, spoken to a spot where things are remembered. "For that child, it should be beautiful. For a poor child, it should be something perfect."

"Another coat or two won't be so hard," Jerry thought. And he went to work.

This daily miracle—being guided—can be ours.[4] If we are willing, and if we stay focused on the true and the kind and the virtuous, the voice will tell us what to do.

22.
Riches for the Right Reasons

Before ye seek for riches, seek ye for the kingdom of God. And after ye have obtained a hope in Christ ye shall obtain riches, if ye seek them; and ye will seek them for the intent to do good. (Jacob 2:18–19.)

A hope in Christ can turn slippery if we don't use our blessings as he intended. "For the sake of retaining a remission of [our] sins," we need to pour out mercy on others.[1] It isn't necessary to be rich in order to do that.[2]

Nan is something of a legend in the care center where she lives. "I was afraid my life was over when I moved in here," she remembers. "But I kind of decided I'd do what I could for the others. I don't have money or other things to give. They don't need that anyway. What I've got is time. I can listen to someone. I can read to someone. I can just sit and be near. Some of these folks don't have visitors. But you know what? I'm here anyway. I might as well just wheel down the hall and visit them myself."

Though we can think of a lot of reasons to be rich, there aren't many reasons from God's point of view—maybe one or two. To switch to his view is a great leap in our maturity. It means the heart—the center of desire—is getting things right.

Cesar and Lilia were itinerant workers who followed the harvest

46

seasons annually, working in three separate states for three separate employers, year after year. And they tried to keep their family of five as active as possible in three different wards. How they longed to settle down. The moving around was not so bad, but they hungered to serve in the Church.

Then Cesar was offered a permanent position with a ward member who had been observing him for some time. One location, one job, one home, and one ward—it was a new world of happiness. Their desire to serve was matched by a temporal blessing.

Whenever we seem a little short on "things," the question is never whether God is generous. Cesar and Lilia and millions of others will testify to that. Said Nephi, "My God will give me, if I ask not amiss."[3] No, generosity is for us, not him, to learn.

Nor is our Father ever confused about what we need. We are the ones who have trouble with that. A real achievement for most of us is simply to "ask not amiss."

For some of us, it is tempting to worry that people will judge us if our temporal things aren't nice. But we ought to think less about that and more about the real judgment. At that day, we won't answer for whether our things were nice but for whether our things did any good.[4]

And that is just what they're for. "The Lord God doth work by means"—things, tools, the materials of a mortal world—"to bring about his great and eternal purposes."[5] And so should we.

23.
EACH PERSON IS PRECIOUS

The one being is as precious in his sight as the other. (Jacob 2:21.)

There is a dangerous tendency for human beings, once they manage some little success, to feel superior to others. Our narrow triumphs may prove temporary. People catch up or fall behind. Rankings change. Because of this, rankings don't matter.

And how can you rank two infinites? Look out across the Indian Ocean, and look out across the Atlantic. Which is most vast and overwhelming? Look out to the universe in one direction and then look in another. Which is most endless and awesome?

Look to any two souls. What would be the folly of saying that one falls short of the other, especially when both are still capable of dramatic change? For each, the future may hold surprises. Which one would be most misled by our silly comparisons? And not only misled but damaged?

When Jacob spoke of this habit of proud comparing, he didn't just say it was futile or absurd. He said that "such things are abominable unto him who created all flesh."[1]

Jacob added that "all flesh is of the dust."[2] The frame of flesh we look upon—and which we may rank or grade somehow—is only a shell.

Bryan, who is a blend of mechanical genius and mischief, thought it would be great to install a big racing engine in the shell of a boxy old car known as the Nash Rambler. He couldn't wait to surprise people who misjudged the car by its body. Last we heard, Bryan was still trying to solve a few technical problems.

Most of us really will underestimate the power of that car, even after he gets it running. We might be even more mistaken if we see it still under construction. But Bryan won't pay attention to our thoughts on the matter. He knows what he's up to.

We might say that our Father's family is a fleet of Ramblers, getting fitted out with amazing power. We could say that it is a great mistake to judge each other, especially since most of us are not completely put together yet. In this we would be right.

But in a way, each of us is also a Bryan. If we see Bryan's car on a shaky test run, we might look at the car and say, "There goes poor old boxy Bryan." We not only misjudged the vehicle, but we have also forgotten that Bryan is not a car. He is the being inside.

The "being" Jacob mentioned is the reality. The rest is decoration and debris. The being inside the shell is the reality. That hidden person isn't just what makes us who we are; it *is* who we are. This is the "being" that is considered so "precious in the sight of God." It is what God sees all along—the part he never stops watching, never stops prizing and loving.

24.
VIRTUE IS WORTH ANY COST

I, the Lord God, delight in the chastity of women. (Jacob 2:28.)

God has made little children to be visual aids. They remind us of what maturity—spiritual maturity—really means. They are heroes for the adults around them.[1] In most homes and villages of the earth, these tiny teachers outnumber the big students. So you would think the students, the stuffy and blind adults of the world, would catch on to the lessons a little better.

One of the most striking truths these little heroes ever teach is portrayed without saying a word. The lesson is radiated. Maybe it could be put into words like these: Purity is beautiful. Or, virtue is noble at any age. Or, innocence is worth any cost.

Perhaps, an innocent adult is more deserving of honor than an innocent child. All children are pure. But a pure and virtuous adult is a treasure to humanity. So it is from the Lord's view of us.

And by what sign might we know how well, or how poorly, a people is doing in these matters? What signal is most telling? The chastity of women.

This may not tell us everything

about the men. But it may tell us if there is any hope for the men.

Virtue, worthy, and *work* come from the same root. The idea is that a thing is worthy or has virtue if it does what it was designed to do—if it works. Ships that are watertight and operate as they should are called "seaworthy."

The virtuous soul is not only clean but can also do its work. We were made for happiness; for peace; for wisdom, judgment, and decision-making; for getting along with others; for detecting needs, giving service, and growing toward the stature of God.

These were the aims of our design. But the equipment is delicate. Great violins are not made of popsicle sticks and duct tape. God made us for exaltation, so he used no cheap, insensitive materials. Only virtue can keep us capable of our greatest possibilities.

With virtue, we have the right stuff. If worthy, the soul works and can even get better. The ship weathers all storms and gets us across the deep.

Some of us know what it is to buy cheap tools. They may look fancy, but watch out. A cheap tool can leave you stranded on the road or the roof. Unworthy ships get part way and leave you on the rocks. Unvirtuous companions and unworthy lives may never arrive where they were headed, because the delicate instruments and sensors and powers of the soul stop working. Worthiness is worth any cost.

Jacob went on to describe the opposite of virtue. He didn't call it maturity or modernity or style. He didn't just call it sin. He described moral unworthiness as it is: death.[2] It can only wreck the possibilities and life of the soul.

Virtue insures the life. Chastity is a sign of hope. No wonder God delights in it.

25.
A Feast for the Firm

I, Jacob, would speak unto you that are pure in heart. Look unto God with firmness of mind, and pray unto him with exceeding faith, and he will console you in your afflictions. . . . O all ye that are pure in heart, lift up your heads and receive the pleasing word of God, and feast upon his love; for ye may, if your minds are firm, forever. (Jacob 3:1–2.)

There are usually people in any group who are living as they should. Not everyone in Jacob's audience needed a wake-up call. Some were not only awake but had been awake a long time. They had been walking a steep hill alone.

The Lord inspired Jacob to send these pure ones a friendly word and a promise of joy. To those who were already clean, the Lord was saying, "I know you. I will stand by you. I intend to welcome you and host you in my home. And until then I will console you."

But for that consolation to be felt, there is a condition. Even the pure need to have firm minds. If we are not willing to accept a kind greeting, we are lost in our sad or lonely thoughts—firmly stuck in our mud. Good news is of little use to those who lack confidence in the newsbearer, and who expect bad news only. If Satan cannot get the righteous to sin, he would at least tempt them to skip the feast.

The Lord is always quiet and gentle in his messages, even when he is expressing his affection—especially then. If we are strictly sad or stoutly self-doubting, how will we accept the Lord's tenderness? We may be turning our head from the nourishment we need. He may have to try another time, when we are more confident in him, when we are more open to a happy theme, when our faith is more firm.

Firmness is purity grown up. It is the mature version of goodness, the deep and dependable result of being pure for a long time and for the long run and under all circumstances.

Firmness isn't showy or brash. It is quiet but unswerving.

Consider those scenes in the sacred record where a prophet is under siege. The cynics wonder at the calm. They hope they have found some weakness in the stranger before them. But the stranger waits without wilting. He is not brash, but he does not bend.[1]

The unsettling sense finally comes to them that they have made a terrible mistake. They are mocking a giant, throwing pebbles at a mountain. The weakness is all theirs.

"Your words have been stout against me, saith the Lord. . . . Ye have said: It is vain to serve God, and what doth it profit that we have kept his ordinances?"[2]

In the world there is a notion that the gospel promises are but empty entertainment for fools, that God is not paying attention, that his word cannot be trusted. Time will tell whose entertainment was empty, and who was foolish.

The pure will see God, but they won't have to wait until then to know the comfort that is a steady stream and the assurance that sometimes surges with unspeakable joy.[3] The feast is already underway.

26.
GROWING IN FAITH

We search the prophets, and we have many revelations and the spirit of prophecy; and having all these witnesses we obtain a hope, and our faith becometh unshaken. (Jacob 4:6.)

Jacob knew what it was to direct the forces of nature by faith. For example, he could report that "the very trees obey us."[1] Certain miracles had come by Jacob's spoken "command." Behind the command was the substance of mighty faith.

By long experience, Jacob knew just how "faith becometh unshaken." (He lived a long time, as suggested by his son's comment in Enos 1:25.) Like all things magnificent and real, faith grows in lawful stages.[2]

To begin, "we search the prophets," which continues through life and takes many forms. For example, there is the story of a certain Lamanite queen.[3]

One day she was stunned by the tragic news that her husband, Lamoni, had suddenly died. She had his body brought into their home. Matters of state must have combined with her grief into a waking nightmare. Nevertheless, there dawned on her the strange impression that her husband was not really dead. And another odd thought: She should summon the heroic Nephite who had recently come to live among them. Ammon came. With little hesitation, he began to teach her the gospel.

She had never met the light-skinned stranger. But she searched his words with her heart and did the honest thing: She believed everything he said. It was a quick turn to the light. It was the beginning of faith at its finest. "There has not been such great faith among all the people of the Nephites."[4]

Nephites grew up with the fundamentals. They knew the basic story. But a Lamanite would have to abandon a ton of tradition for every pound of gospel truth. After searching a moment, she did not hesitate.

Even her husband, whose own faith was so striking, had needed a ramp to belief. He had needed the dramatic evidence that Ammon was reliable, a careful lesson in history, and a summary of the plan of redemption before staking everything on Ammon's words. The queen required nothing but a phrase: "He is not dead, but he sleepeth in God."[5] A single note from the right instrument was all the music she needed.

Like training wheels on a bicycle, the prophets get us started. The more we search, the more we taste the spirit of revelation. Another stage unfolds—what Jacob describes as "many revelations and the spirit of prophecy."

At what stage are we now: searching the prophets; or many revelations; or faith unshaken? Perhaps the early part. We will find that faith grows much as the morning dew appears on the grass, or as the hour hand creeps surely around the clock every twelve hours. The movement is too slow for the human eye. But now and then we check it, and there it is. Our capacity really is growing, the heavens really are responding to our needs. Our faith is becoming mighty.

27.
Inspiration We Can Understand

The Spirit speaketh the truth and lieth not. Wherefore, it speaketh of things as they really are, and of things as they really will be; wherefore, these things are manifested unto us plainly. (Jacob 4:13.)

"I'm a little confused," Semisi muttered. His eyes connected with the bishop's a moment and then focused on the portrait of the First Presidency. "I wish I had the prophet's ears."

"The prophet's ears?" the bishop asked.

"Sure." Semisi shrugged. "He doesn't have trouble hearing what the Lord says to him!"

The bishop leaned forward and smiled. "And so you think the Lord is trying to tell you whether to marry Natasha, and you just can't hear what he's saying?" The strapping Tongan returned missionary nodded slowly. "Can I just ask you a few questions?" the bishop asked. Semisi nodded again. "Didn't you tell us once that there were many times on your mission when you knew you were being guided by the Spirit?"

"Yeah, and a lot of other times when I didn't even notice it was happening!"

"And wasn't it you and your home-teaching companion that had a feeling you should take two cars on your home-teaching route a couple of months ago?"

Semisi smiled. "We didn't know

why, but we just had this definite feeling, and when we got to our last family, we found out their car was broke down, and so we could leave my car with them for the week. It was so great, Bishop."

"Yes, and it was so clear, right?" Semisi looked puzzled. "The impression, the inspiration. It was clear, right?" Semisi nodded. "And when you taught your Primary lesson last Sunday, was it hard for you to know what to teach the children?"

"No. I was prepared, and the Spirit came, and I felt I should sort of stress certain things."

"Would you grab that Book of Mormon and turn to 2 Nephi 31? I think it's verse 3."

Semisi read the verse. "Wow, Bishop, how'd you remember about that one?"

"Well, I have to look it up now and then myself. See what Nephi says there? 'My soul delighteth in plainness.' I think that kind of rubbed off on him from all his contact with the Lord. He says, 'For after this manner doth the Lord God work.' That's the Lord's manner, Semisi. When he gives us direction, it's always plain enough to understand."

Semisi was quiet for several seconds as the bishop sat back and waited. "So, when it's time for me to know about Natasha, it will be just as clear as the answers I got on my mission . . ."

"Or just as definite as the prompting you got that day home teaching, or . . ."

"Or when I know what to say to the Primary children, right?"

"The Lord specializes in communication, Semisi. When he sends us an answer, he knows how to make us understand."

57

28.
SAVING THOSE WHO WANDER

The Lord of the vineyard caused that it should be digged about, and pruned, and nourished, saying unto his servant: It grieveth me that I should lose this tree; wherefore, . . . I have done this thing. . . . And he beheld . . . that it had brought forth much fruit; and he beheld also that it was good. And he said . . . this long time have I nourished it, and it hath brought forth much fruit. (Jacob 5:11, 20.)

When Jacob gave us the allegory of the olive tree, he wasn't trying to write the biggest chapter in history. He was trying to answer one of the biggest questions in history: How can a wanderer ever come home? Or, as he said it after speaking of a certain people who had rejected the Foundation, "How is it possible that these . . . can ever build upon it?" He used the long allegory to "unfold this mystery."[1]

The length of Jacob's answer says a lot about how patient God must be as he ministers to his more distracted or rebellious children. Sick and fruitless trees are not renewed in one season, and so it is with sick and fruitless souls. Pruning, grafting, digging, and nourishing take time. They are all forms of really caring.[2]

One these caring acts—nourishing—is simple enough for us to do among wanderers.

Pruning removes the long, lofty, overreaching arms that grab up all the substance they can, that overtax the roots that give them life, that "corrupt" the whole vineyard.[3] Only God can wisely prune excesses from the lives of his children.

Grafting families and relationships around, separating here and merging there—this is another process that none but God can manage.

Digging is how the Gardener softens and breaks the soil. We remember that the soil is a symbol for the soul, the heart that harbors the seed at first and fosters the roots later on.[4] We can hardly expect anyone but him to do such things with a heart.[5]

But as the Gardener does his part, caring assistants can add nutrients to the soil.

A caring mother and father had just heard a report of some disappointing behavior on the part of their son. Somewhat stunned, they sat late one night deciding what to do. "Shall we talk to him?" the father wondered. His wife was silent a while and finally answered, "Do you think it will help?"

"I don't know. But we had better try. I just wish I knew what words to say."

Yes, they will need to say something. In this, they are something like the wise Eternal Father. But he has just exactly the right words, designed to nourish, cleanse, and heal his offspring, even the wanderers who stumble and misbehave. He planned all along that every human soul would need to be "nourished by the good word of God."[6]

As soil meets the demands of growing plants and trees, it loses richness. Nutrients have to be added back in. Our souls are like that. The pressures of life deplete us. We were not designed to go through the years, or even the days, without being nourished again and again. Jacob unfolded the "mystery." The Lord's nutrients are mixed in with his word.

29.
SOARING AMID DARK CLOUDS

There are many among us who have many revelations, for they are not all stiffnecked. And as many as are not stiffnecked and have faith, have communion with the Holy Spirit, which maketh manifest unto the children of men, according to their faith. (Jarom 1:4.)

Jens is a burly man. The bushy hair, broad smile, and booming voice give him extra size. This makes his wife, Kara, seem all the more petite and queenly. They were speaking this day in sacrament meeting. As Kara mentioned that the branch president had asked them to speak about enduring trials, the congregation became very quiet.

Everyone knew that Jens had lost his business to a terrible downturn in the economy a year before. They had moved their family from a comfortable home to a small apartment. They were still in the branch boundaries, so Jens continued on as Young Men's president, still full of energy and humor.

Everyone knew of Kara's bout with cancer, a fight she was not winning at the moment. She was more frail than ever. But she still served as Primary chorister. If possible, her countenance shone brighter and her voice sang sweeter than before.

"A few of you," she was saying, "have asked how we stay cheerful." She turned and nodded at the branch president, who had asked this question more than once. "But of course, you know, don't you? It is the blessing we all have. When we joined the Church, we received the Holy Ghost. When Jens lost everything he had built up for years, he didn't lose the Holy Ghost. When we lost our house, we didn't lose our sweet home evenings. We lost many possessions, but not the Church, or the truth."

Kara's voice wavered a bit. She stood a little taller, smiled, and added, "I haven't been feeling very well lately, but I have not felt abandoned by the Lord. I feel his presence even more than before. He has made our testimonies stronger, and he has taught us and our children. What a great year this has been for us spiritually."

So it was with another people about 2,000 years before. The Nephites were in a time of alarm, and yet they were not alarmed. While war loomed more and more likely, "those who were faithful in keeping the commandments of the Lord were delivered at all times. . . . Behold there never was a happier time among the people of Nephi."[1]

The statement we have quoted from Jarom's writings was made in the midst of turmoil, wickedness, and war. And yet there were "many" people in Jarom's day like Jens and Kara of our day. They had "communion"—comfort, support, closeness—"with the Holy Spirit." Any of those people, speaking in a sacrament meeting, might have said what Kara said. Though they might lose all else, they need not lose that Spirit.

30.
THE WHOLE SOUL

I would that ye should come unto Christ, who is the Holy One of Israel, and partake of his salvation, and the power of his redemption. Yea, come unto him, and offer your whole souls as an offering unto him, and continue in fasting and praying, and endure to the end; and as the Lord liveth ye will be saved. (Omni 1:26.)

The postman dropped off the day's mail at the shoe repair shop and said, "Hey, I wonder if you could put a little patch on my soles."

"Little patch?" the shoemaker answered. "Those are work shoes, aren't they?"

"Sure, but the hole isn't big. Can't you just do a cheap job, just fix a part of the sole?"

"Nope, not if you're planning to use this in real life. I'll have to do the whole thing. A part will just leak and fall apart."

Another man walked into an auto repair and said, "There's a problem with the steering on this car. I wonder if I could just leave the steering wheel."

"Sorry, sir," replied the mechanic. "I'll need the whole car. It all kind of fits together, you know."

A golf instructor was explaining that a perfect swing involves the whole body. "Form is head to toe," was his slogan.

"I just want to work on this one arm for now," his student complained. "Nothing else."

"I'm afraid it wouldn't do much

good to just work on one arm and ignore the rest of your form. It all has to work together."

Unlike lesser friends, Christ fixes everything if we let him. He can't accept a part isolated from the rest. All the departments work together or they don't work at all. He doesn't do half souls.[1] One reason Christ is called the "Holy One" may be that he redeems "whole" persons.

The Holy One will redeem a whole soul if it is offered to him.

When he spoke to the survivors after a great destruction, he invited them to get serious about their membership in the Church.[2] Yes, they had been the "more righteous part" of society. But they had been holding back.[3] They had been caught up in cultural compromises. They hadn't given their whole souls.

King Benjamin said we'd better get the name of Christ "written always" in our hearts.[4] How do we go about remembering anyone all the time? Without love, it's impossible. With love, it's impossible to forget.

If we find our love a bit weak, we can use the method proposed in our promise: "continue in fasting and praying"—the perfect way to unclog a soul and free it up to be given.

It is the partial, clogged offering that gets technical and difficult. The unclogged soul can do the simple, uncomplicated thing. It can be totally loyal. We are loyal, not simply because the Holy One will win, but also because he is worthy—a true friend seeking no advantage for himself. He gives his whole soul to us. For those who return that gift, salvation is not just a possibility.

31.

USING THE VERY WORDS

Were it not for these plates,
which contain these records and
these commandments, we must
have suffered in ignorance, even
at this present time, not
knowing the mysteries of God.
(Mosiah 1:3.)

We are only a dozen verses into the Book of Mormon when we are taught this lesson by Lehi's experience: "As he read, he was filled with the Spirit of the Lord."[1]

Benjamin, the king and prophet, sought that blessing for his family from the time his sons were little. They didn't "become men of understanding" by accident. Benjamin knew that the words on the brass plates had been "delivered them by the hand of the Lord" for some towering purpose, so he used them at home.[2]

Every family should not just have the records. They should also be able to say, "We have them before our eyes."[3] It is not the ideas of God, or his general notions, but his very words that we are to ponder. Mere ideas float and drift if they are not engraved on metal or pressed onto a page.

"Were it not for these plates," the essentials would have been lost. The best efforts and care of devoted parents, without scripture, are not enough to save their children. Even Lehi himself could not have done it, Benjamin said, "except it were for the help of these plates."[4]

No wonder the word of God is worth trading life itself to preserve, translate, and publish for parents everywhere. And if it is so crucial to get it that far in its journey, surely it is worth the trouble to take it the last step or two.

What step or two? It must be studied and lived, most of all at home. That is where hearts are fed and lives are built. Someone at home needs to open the expensive gift.

Is it worth as much to a parent to use the gift as it was to some prophet or missionary or teacher or pioneer to deliver it? For that forerunner, it meant giving up livelihood, comfort, time, personal plans—or life itself—to take the written words of God some small leg of the journey from heaven. Once the precious cargo arrives and is published, it may cost the price of a few meals to buy a nicely bound copy. But even then, the unwrapping hasn't begun.

It is unveiled when time is set aside, when eyes and minds are opened, when the words are read and pages are turned, when thoughts are stirred for long enough to become complete thoughts, to become decisions. That is when conscience kneels before new light, when covenants are transformed into live deeds.

If enough time will be spent with those words, faith can be exerted and sins can be dropped along the trail. And these things being done, the pages can be turned again and the sanctifying process repeat itself day by day, year after year, building ever more light to our last breath. That is how the gift becomes worth what it cost.

32.
IT ALL COUNTS

This mortal shall put on immortality, and this corruption shall put on incorruption, and shall be brought to stand before the bar of God, to be judged of him according to their works whether they be good or whether they be evil. (Mosiah 16:10.)

The warning is that we will be judged for doing wrong. The promise is that we will be judged for doing right.

Occasionally we see a news clip recorded by a security camera. For example, right on film an angry robber suddenly threatens an innocent woman who happens to be present. It looks as if he may even take her life. But something surprising happens, more interesting and valuable than catching a crime on film.

Another innocent woman springs out of nowhere and shoves the bad guy to the floor. In a few seconds that man has people all over him. The conquerors are piled on his legs and arms and chest, talking with each other as if they were old friends, soothing the would-be victim and complimenting the hero as they wait for the police to arrive.

That lady who jumped into the tense scene, willing to take a bullet for a stranger, was seen by more than cameras and bystanders and TV viewers.

"If their works were good in this life, and the desires of their hearts were good, . . . they should also, at the last day, be restored unto that which is good."[1]

It is all about doing, or trying mightily to do. No one is a bystander here; all can act and strive to act. Life—in the long run, at least—is fair and more than fair. We will finally reach the heights of virtue we were always climbing to reach.[2]

A man sat looking out the back window, watching his grandchildren play together. One of them came into the house for a drink of water and was surprised to see Grandpa sitting there. "Have you been watching to see if we were being bad, Grandpa?" the child asked.

"No, not at all," he answered. "I just like to watch you being good." He is like some employers, who like to watch security videos not to catch bad guys but to see their employees doing a good job. Our Father wants to witness the best in us.

When we come before him, we will be fine and noble in appearance; immortal, perfect, and well—splendid and superhuman. What could mar the beauty of this reunion scene? The memory of disloyalties lived in the flesh, or of treason that once lurked in the heart.

Such remorse can be avoided. We can both repent and prepent, you might say. We can repair our mistakes and take a wide path around ever repeating them. In creating a record bright with solid good, we may become bright with good ourselves.

We will have the light we wanted. We may not be handed what we only casually approved. But we will have what we fought for, what we wrought out and sought.

No good work will be overlooked in the judgment. It will be so for every person who ever lived and did any good thing.[3]

33.
HE NOTICES IMMEDIATELY

He never doth vary from that which he hath said; therefore, if ye do keep his commandments he doth bless you and prosper you. . . . He doth require that ye should do as he hath commanded you; for which if ye do, he doth immediately bless you. (Mosiah 2:22, 24.)

In the book of Alma, we read of the Zoramites. They came so close to the point of no return that a prophet was sent on a last mission to reclaim them. One of the pleasant surprises in Book of Mormon history is that Alma's mission to the Zoramites was a success, at least among the poor in their city.[1] But for the others, the road led downward from that time on.[2]

As time was running out for these people, Alma spoke urgently. They had to act right away. "Now is the time and the day of your salvation," he said. It was one of those moments that might bring out the best in people.

Alma made them an unusual promise: If they would act immediately, God would too. "If ye will repent and harden not your hearts, immediately shall the great plan of redemption be brought about unto you."[3]

For those who did act, the Lord responded with a mighty hand, just as the prophet said he would. Soon these people had left poverty and persecution behind. They were relocated to a land full of opportunity, welcomed by generous new friends.[4]

The Lord doesn't always turn things around so quickly. In fact, he doesn't usually. But there are two things he always does: He always notices our obedience right away, and he always responds to our obedience as quickly as he says he will.

If he does not rush to an action that we can see with our poor eyes, he is certainly never sluggish or sleepy, either. His hand, whether moving with the speed of lightning or with the speed of a glacier, is awesome in power. (He isn't really slow as a glacier. But still, that comparison comes to mind.) He is a being of action, but he isn't going for speed. He isn't trying to dazzle anyone. He keeps promises with perfect integrity and perfect timing.

We can't blame the Lord for being concerned about our integrity and timing. He knows that slow obedience will likely mean no obedience.[5]

Lamoni thought Ammon was a divine being because of the way he followed up on things. We expect God to keep promises the way he does everything: perfectly.[6]

The speed philosophy works for some things and ruins others. We like speedy delivery when we pay for something and speedy payment when we deliver something. But we don't like bread that is cooked too fast, or anesthesia that wears off too fast. We like responsive brakes, because when it comes to stopping at the edge of a cliff, timing is everything. But we don't want to be skidding to a halt at every stop sign.

We will have to let the Lord mix his glacial timing with his colossal integrity. Steadily, irresistibly, he does what he says he will do. We cannot rush him. And nothing can slow him down.

34.
THE DEBTS
ARE PAID BY
A GOD

*God himself shall come down
among the children of men, and
shall redeem his people.
(Mosiah 15:1.)*

A Church film called *Testaments* portrayed the visit of Christ to Book of Mormon people. The story was set in the ancient Mayan culture of Central America. When Delora saw the film, she had a desire to visit the places depicted there.

And now Delora was visiting those very jungles. As she sat on the wall of a great stone "ball court," the guide said the place dated to about 150 B.C. She looked through her Book of Mormon to find something from that period and came across the story of Abinadi speaking to the corrupt court of King Noah. There in Mosiah 15 were the prophet's words that "God himself" would come and "redeem his people." She wondered why the king and his priests were so offended at such a beautiful doctrine.

She tried to picture Abinadi in surroundings like these, and she considered the intense ball game that historians now called "Poc-de-Poc" because of the sound of a heavy latex ball bouncing off stone surfaces and human chests and legs. The guide explained that a nationwide tournament was held each year in ancient times. The championship game would decide which player in all the land was the national hero. The heart would then be cut from this athlete's chest and offered up to the angry Mayan gods. The game was their way of finding the greatest heart in the land.

Someone in Delora's group asked, "But why would anyone try to be the 'Most Valuable Player' if it meant he would be sacrificed?"

A retired coach in the group laughed and said, "You don't know the athletes I've known. Some will do anything, and I mean anything, to be the best."

The guide added, "You also have to know the Mayans. To have the greatest heart was the highest honor. The hero died for all the people. He was guaranteed eternal life."

Delora thought of what a shock it would be to have Abinadi or some other prophet come along and say that none of these traditions would work. She looked at the verse in Mosiah again. God himself would do it, not a man. She guessed at what Abinadi's words meant to them. "Your mean old deities would never do this. But the living God is going to come and be the hero. Your traditions are all wrong. Your horrible human sacrifices aren't doing a bit of good. Your 'priests' are all frauds."

Since that afternoon in the ruins of a Mayan ball court, Delora has realized that every culture, ancient or modern, needs to realize who the real Hero is.

Speaking to an audience something like Abinadi's, Alma declared, "It shall not be a human sacrifice; but it must be an infinite and eternal sacrifice."[1] A regular human will never do. The "God of nature" must suffer.[2] Not one sacrifice each year, but just one "great and last" sacrifice in all eternity.

35.
THE HEIRS ARE THE ONES WHO LISTEN

Whosoever has heard the words of the prophets, yea, all the holy prophets who have prophesied concerning the coming of the Lord—I say unto you, that all those who have hearkened unto their words, and believed that the Lord would redeem his people, and have looked forward to that day for a remission of their sins, I say unto you, that these are his seed, or they are the heirs of the kingdom of God. (Mosiah 15:11.)

In an elders quorum meeting, the teacher was quoting from Nephi's prayer: "O Lord, wilt thou encircle me around in the robe of thy righteousness! O Lord, wilt thou make a way for mine escape before mine enemies!"[1] One of the quorum members suddenly sat up as if someone had poked him in the back. The teacher stopped and said, "Nabil, are you all right?"

Nabil was a Christian Arab who had recently joined the Church during his studies at an American university. "I'm all right, but I didn't notice those words when I read the Book of Mormon a few months ago."

"Welcome to the club," someone called out. "I've been in the Church my whole life, and I don't remember them either."

After a bit of laughter, the teacher asked Nabil why the words struck him so. "Because there is an ancient robe ceremony that people in the Near East have had for many centuries." Nabil now had everyone's attention as he continued. "It is used to bring people into the clan. The robe is wrapped around the husband and wife when they marry, or around the parents and a new baby at birth."

"So this happened to you?" the teacher asked.

"Of course," Nabil answered. "But I am thinking of a family story from a long time ago, when someone came into the camp of one of my ancestors and asked for protection. Some kind of enemy was after him. My ancestor held a long council. The decision was to let the man be a member of the family. It was a very rare thing. And difficult."

"Because that man's enemies now became the enemies of this whole clan?"

"Yes. And he would be a full member of the family. He would even be an heir."

"Inherit wealth right along with any other child?" the teacher asked with amazement.

"Exactly," Nabil responded. "The man was already a faithful friend to one of the sons. That made the difference. So they adopted him. The robe was wrapped around him, the ceremony took place, and he was part of the family from then on."

After a silence, the teacher read the words again. "Wilt thou encircle me around in the robe of thy righteousness! Wilt thou make a way for mine escape before mine enemies!"

Nephi wanted to be protected and treated like a son. He wanted the Savior to be like a father. Not just a brother or a teacher or a leader, but more like a father.

How do we enter into that robe from Christ and become an heir? The promise is clear. When he sends a prophet, hear that prophet, love the words of that prophet, obey that prophet. The prophets are already good sons in the family. Be their faithful friends and become an heir with them.[2]

36.
MODEST LEADERS HAVE POWER

The priests were not to depend upon the people for their support; but for their labor they were to receive the grace of God, that they might wax strong in the Spirit, having the knowledge of God, that they might teach with power and authority from God. (Mosiah 18:26.)

The modest, unselfish leader is promised the perfect rate of pay, measured as influence. He or she will find, just when it is needed, the power to inspire and lift. Fortunately, this doesn't require us to please mankind. In fact, the Lord doesn't mind placing his servants where they won't be noticed. Of course, we know where they are: in his hand. We sense it, but we may not see it. He loves the modest-but-useful servant.

"In the shadow of his hand hath he hid me, . . . and said unto me: Thou art my servant."[1]

The mouthpiece he is likely to inspire is the modest one, the one not trying to sound grand, and who doesn't consider himself superior in some way.[2]

"I have put my words in thy mouth, and have covered thee in the shadow of mine hand."[3]

King Benjamin was a modest and powerful servant. At the close of life, he could "answer a clear conscience."[4] How? It was his life of service. He had viewed his resources merely as the means to serve.[5] He had worn himself out in service.[6] Someone might say, "He would have worn out eventually anyway." The question is not if we will wear out, but in what way we choose to wear out. How will we use up our precious strength and time? How will we "spend" our lives?

The modest servant lies down tired at the end of a day, knowing that the day was spent doing just what God intended. How could you feel badly about a day like that, no matter what went wrong? Benjamin lay down in peace each evening for thousands of days and then did so at the end of his life.

The modest leader represents the Lord but knows when to represent the people as well. The brother of Jared went before the Lord in behalf of his people. We notice in one of his prayers how often he uses the words "us" and "we" and "our." For example:

"O Lord, thou hast said that *we* must be encompassed about by the floods. . . . *We* know that thou art holy and dwellest in the heavens, and that *we* are unworthy before thee; because of the fall *our* natures have become evil continually; nevertheless, O Lord, thou hast given *us* a commandment that *we* must call upon thee, that from thee *we* may receive according to *our* desires.[7]

This continues, and he finally says, "*We* know that thou art able to show forth great power."[8] He was expressing the faith of his people.

What was the result of this modest praying? What was the result of Benjamin's modest ministry? In one case, a nation was born. In the other case, a nation was reborn. Such is the result of modest service.[9]

37.
He Takes His Church Seriously

And he that will hear my voice shall be my sheep; and him shall ye receive into the church, and him will I also receive. (Mosiah 26:21.)

As the new leader of the Church in Zarahemla, Alma had a big problem. While there were many faithful members, there were also a certain number who rebelled.[1] He inquired of the Lord, "for he feared that he should do wrong" in the action he would take. The answer was a wonderful revelation about the purpose of Church membership.[2]

And that would be the perfect guide. By knowing the Lord's purpose in having a church to begin with, Alma could make wise decisions about church membership.

What is the Church for, anyway? Is it a building? A way of life? A culture? A righteous sort of club? Notice a few phrases from the revelation:

"They shall be *my* people."[3] "In *my* name shall they be called; and they are *mine*."[4] "Thou . . . shalt gather together *my* sheep."[5] "He that will hear *my* voice shall be *my* sheep; . . . him will *I* also receive."[6] "This is *my* church."[7] "Whomsoever ye receive shall believe in *my* name; and him will *I* freely forgive."[8]

So it continues for many verses.

The Savior takes personally every element and every member of his Church. The revelation seems to say that the Church is for people who care about Christ. It is many other things, but these are secondary. Above all, the Church is for the friends of Christ.[9] Through his Church, they have his voice, his closeness, and the association of his other friends.[10]

Knowing this, Alma could guide the Church through this difficult time.[11]

Those who wanted to be identified with Christ, who wanted to be his people and do his will, remained. Those who were opposed to the shepherd were not required to stay in the fold.[12]

It means a lot when the Church members are "called the people of God," because it is God himself who chooses to call them that.[13] He likes to call us his.

So, what does it mean to have our names in the Church record? It means everything. We are officially listed as the friends of Christ.[14] For now, we don't worry about whether the list is accurate. Many names will yet be added. Someday the list will be complete. But we are honored to be there. We want to stay on that list forever.

What holds the Church together? What ensures that the church will be "one fold"? Just this: the shepherd.[15] We are one fold because every one of us is interested in exactly the same shepherd. We are together because we gather around him. He holds on to those who hold on to his Church.

38.
LIVING PROPHETS AND NEW LIFE

What is the cause of their being loosed from the bands of death, yea, and also the chains of hell? Behold, I can tell you—did not my father Alma believe in the words which were delivered by the mouth of Abinadi? And was he not a holy prophet? Did he not speak the words of God, and my father Alma believe them? And according to his faith there was a mighty change wrought in his heart. (Alma 5:10–12.)

We can't make "a mighty change of heart" on our own power. It occurs in a place unseen by the natural eye, a place impossible for the natural man to reach. The heart is where desires are formed and fed and kept. Like merely changing the angle of a ship's rudder or sail, adjusting the angle of the front wheel of a bicycle, or tugging slightly on the reins of a well-trained horse, a better angle or special tug in the heart transforms a life. Hidden adjustments in desire change our destination.

What caused this to happen to the people of King Benjamin? What had they been doing just before it happened? They hadn't been reading a book or attending a great concert. Such things can reassure and teach and inspire and confirm, but they do not permanently change hearts. The people had just been listening to a living prophet. They believed everything he said. Something changed inside, something definite they could feel. They weren't suddenly perfect, for that change takes years or decades or centuries. But the rudder had been set to a new and better angle.

"We have no more disposition to do evil, but to do good continually." It happened in that spot no human can see or adjust. Only a force potent enough to be called "omnipotent" could reach that deep and turn the dial. "The Spirit of the Lord Omnipotent . . . has wrought a mighty change in us."[1]

The same had been true of Alma the Elder. Just before the change that altered him, what had he been doing? Listening to a prophet. The promise we have quoted says this: "Did he not speak the words of God, and my father Alma believe them? And according to his faith there was a mighty change wrought in his heart."

That was only the beginning. A cascade of changes then took place as Alma was called to teach others. Those others believed him as he had believed Abinadi (and as Abinadi must have believed some prophet before that). The result was, "a mighty change was also wrought in their hearts."[2]

When we believe in the words of one who speaks for the Lord, a healing power is quietly, invisibly called down upon the heart. We cannot make a mighty change on our own power, but we can qualify for it. We can find a prophet and believe him.

Sometimes the prophet finds us. Zoram was minding his own business one night when someone that seemed a lot like Laban came and asked in a voice that seemed a lot like Laban's voice to join him in taking the brass plates for a little walk. Perhaps Zoram had been hoping or praying for a mighty change in his life, but in any case that's how it turned out. A prophet named Nephi, and another named Lehi, found him. He believed, he changed, he was blessed.[3]

39.
REPENTING INTO HIS ARMS

Behold, he sendeth an invitation unto all men, for the arms of mercy are extended towards them, and he saith: Repent, and I will receive you. (Alma 5:33.)

Marni is a four-year-old bundle of energy and assertiveness. She shows no fear. She doesn't obey too many rules. She doesn't mean to terrorize anyone, but other humans[1] in the neighborhood avoid her a lot of the time. She has a tantrum now and then. She finds it hard to say "I'm sorry." After all, she is never, never wrong.

Of course, there is another side to Marni. She is a loving girl and wants to be good. Her mother says, "Other people don't see what I call the Marni Meltdown. Like when it finally hits Marni that she has done something wrong, she waits until she's alone with me and does a U-turn. She just melts into my arms in tears, asking to be forgiven."

How can you not open your arms to a child in meltdown?

The snow and ice in the mountains give life only when touched by the warmth of spring. The raw ore can be neither purified nor shaped until it is willing to melt.

The promise is that the Lord will absolutely, without hesitation, open his great, merciful arms to each person who repents.[2]

He opened his arms to Zeezrom. This hard-bitten, worldly, dishonest man had at one time insisted that he was never, never in the wrong. When he tried to embarrass Alma and Amulek, he was the embarrassed one. Zeezrom learned that he had hardly ever been right. It was a repentance meltdown. The repentance brought healing.[3] Zeezrom was received into the arms of mercy. In a few days' time, he had made a permanent U-turn. He is later mentioned in a list of missionaries.[4]

Another in that list was Corianton. At the time of that mission, his U-turn was still ahead. He was a weak and arrogant missionary. His public contempt for righteousness brought discredit upon the Church, for he was a son of the prophet Alma. The "poor example" contributed to a war that cost innumerable lives. But sometime after that first mission, Corianton passed through a season of repentance and found his place in the arms of Christ. The U-turn may have taken him a while. Meltdowns are sometimes better if they are slow.[5]

Before the embrace comes the voice. The Shepherd calls into the heart, asking for simple repentance. Everyone knows the voice, however dimly.[6] It is beckoning right this minute.[7]

Why does the Shepherd do it? He got into this line of work because he loves it. He loves the sheep. He draws so close to them at times that a fire finds its way from him to the repentant person, and the fire makes things new.[8] Now and always, he sincerely wants to embrace us. Our repentance gives him just the excuse he is looking for.[9]

40.
PROMISES TO THE LAMANITES

There are many promises which are extended to the Lamanites; . . . the Lord will be merciful unto them and prolong their existence in the land. And at some period of time they will be brought to believe in his word, and to know of the incorrectness of the traditions of their fathers; and many of them will be saved. (Alma 9:16–17.)

ou know what?" Ruthie's daddy said. "You look like an Indian Princess." She checked the mirror. Daddy was right. From then on, she was the heir of Pocahontas.

You never knew when Princess Ruthie would turn up missing from a picnic—off the forest path looking for wildlife, or in a tree just above you. After she had watched you in royal silence long enough, she would come lighting down from a branch or bounding out of a bush. She would say something solemn: "I have escaped from my enemies," or "I must find my people," or "I am here to rescue you." It was always nice to have her back.

Ruthie was not alone in her fascination for Lamanites, whether of the Americas or the islands of the sea. It is as if God planted in us this interest for a mistreated and misunderstood people. Perhaps he would do this because of a premortal nobility and a future glory. Perhaps it is in answer to the prayers of Lehi and Sariah.

Enos, grandson to Lehi, tells us of his own prayers. Like other Nephite prophets, he pled that the Lamanites of the future would be reclaimed, but also that this miracle might come by the Nephite scriptures. "I prayed . . . many long strugglings for my brethren, the Lamanites. . . . I did cry unto God that he would preserve the records; and he covenanted with me that he would bring them forth unto the Lamanites."[1]

It is a strange story. The Lamanites would destroy an old enemy, the Nephites, and then sink into apostasy. They would come under the rule of cruel strangers. Old enemies would be replaced by enemies much worse. And then a book written by those bygone Nephites would be found and translated by a prophet belonging to neither family.

As the Lamanites honor this book, they rise out of oppression. They are principal partners in building up the Kingdom of God on earth. Enos and others prayed that it would be so. Before our eyes the prayers are answered.[2] The royalty reappears—to return, reclaim, even to rescue.

But why are they blessed in this way? "Because of their steadfastness when they do believe, . . . because of their firmness when they are once enlightened, behold, the Lord shall bless them."[3]

For example, there was a time mentioned in 3 Nephi when "the church was broken up in all the land save it were among a few of the Lamanites who were converted unto the true faith; and they would not depart from it."[4] It is difficult to find an account of any Lamanite in ancient history who ever fell away after being converted. With the Lord, firmness counts for a lot. And it counts for a very, very long time.

41.
WE WILL STAND BEFORE HIM

The spirit and the body shall be reunited again in its perfect form . . . and we shall be brought to stand before God, knowing even as we know now, and have a bright recollection. (Alma 11:43.)

We will meet with the Judge outside a gate. The decision will be whether the celestial land will be our home.[1] A wise old prophet said, "It is better that a man should be judged of God than of man."[2]

As he stands there in his perfection before us, we too will have a certain perfection. We will have radiant health. Our bodies will be timeless and perfect.

And if we are going to have bright recollection, it might as well be of a shiny life. If we are going to be physically fit, it would be a shame to feel aghast at the things we remember. It would be a shame to be filled with shame.

The Messiah has been working for a long time to get everything and everyone ready. Even to plan such a thing was a wonder of genius and generosity. "How great the goodness of our God, who prepareth a way for our escape from the grasp of this awful monster."[3]

The worst monsters of nature or fiction are not only vicious but also inescapable. Like the crocodiles of Central America—lightning fast, enormous jaws, sharp teeth, hungry.

And like death, unslayable—except before the One Great Knight, the Messiah.

What a Hero. We make our escape by his "way of deliverance," while he suffers in order to slay the monster once and for all.[4]

Captain Berg looked himself over in the mirror, eyeing every detail of his uniform. He was being considered for command of a ship—not a large ship, but his first. He had been dreaming of this since he was a boy. After all the work, the interview was only twenty minutes away. "So, the preparations are over," he thought. "But I am ready."

A moment like this is coming for everyone. Twenty minutes before that interview, we will be about through with our preparations. Even now we can look at our hands and say, "These are the hands." We can look in the mirror and say, "With these eyes I will see him." We can touch our knees and say, "With these I will kneel." But we must also ask, "What memories will I bring before him?"[5]

In his glory, he is like a great lamp, a living searchlight under which no detail can be hidden. The brightness will reveal all about him, and all about us.[6] Everything that could possibly be flattering about us will be pointed out by our Judge. "The righteous shall have a perfect knowledge of their enjoyment, and their righteousness."[7]

"I rejoice in the day when my mortal shall put on immortality, and shall stand before him; then shall I see his face with pleasure, and he will say unto me: Come unto me, ye blessed."[8]

42.
REVELATION FOR THE HUNGRY HEART

He that will not harden his heart, to him is given the greater portion of the word, until it is given unto him to know the mysteries of God until he know them in full. (Alma 12:10.)

Sixteen-year-old Denny looked out at the members of his ward. "I hope it's all right to tell a story about three little pigs in sacrament meeting." Several adults smiled; children looked up from their quiet books and stared. Denny continued, "The bishop asked me to talk about learning the gospel. So here it goes.

"Before the pigs got to be teenagers and tried to build their own houses, they were just babies, all the same size. But one pig ate all the time, and he got big like a brick. Another pig ate sometimes, and he wasn't so big—more like a stick. But the third pig hardly ever ate, and he turned out to be built like a piece of straw. When the little puppy wolves down the street would barely puff on him, he would fall right over.

"So if you don't eat, you turn out to be a runt. If you don't have spiritual food every day, you don't learn the gospel. When you grow up, the devil can just blow you down."

Later, during Gospel Doctrine class, the teacher read from the Sermon at the Temple, 3 Nephi 12:6: "Blessed are all they who do hunger

86

and thirst after righteousness, for they shall be filled with the Holy Ghost."

"Okay," the teacher asked, "what's the principle here?"

"I think I know," one man said. "I know because I was a runt for many years." The teacher, along with others, looked puzzled. "You know, like the pig we heard about in sacrament meeting, the one that didn't eat. That was me, the one in my family who never took an interest in the scriptures, who never paid attention in classes.

"When I got around to going on a mission, I noticed that my other family members had more spiritual experiences than I did. They had a better grip on life, and so on. So I wondered why. Then in the mission field I realized one day that the people who got strong testimonies of the Book of Mormon and the Church were the hungry ones, like Jesus said.

"And it hit me that my family members were like those people, and I was like the other investigators who never read because they didn't care. They didn't show up at Church meetings if it wasn't convenient. And so they weren't too quick to get a testimony.

"I decided I didn't want to be that way anymore. The more I worked at studying, the hungrier I got. I started to really feel the Holy Ghost. I understood things that didn't mean anything to me before. I could really teach because I really understood."

The promise is that if we keep hungering, we will keep being fed light and truth. Then nothing can blow us, or our houses, down.

43.
BEING LED AWAY FROM TEMPTATION

I wish from the inmost part of my heart, yea, with great anxiety even unto pain, . . . that ye would humble yourselves before the Lord, and call on his holy name, and watch and pray continually, that ye may not be tempted above that which ye can bear. (Alma 13:27–28.)

Not all depression is a habit of mind, but for Kristy it was. Counseling had helped, mostly to help her see how severe her habit was. Medication had helped for a while.

But the old reflexes—the old patterns and beliefs, the old temptation to be a victim, the unhappy but long-cultivated role—eventually came back.

It was a comment from her home teacher, Brother Bennett, that convinced her she should pray. "Not too many people in the ward know this," he had said during one of his visits, "but I was an alcoholic for many years." Kristy thought how refined and pure this elderly man seemed. Brother Bennett waited and let this information sink in.

"It was bad. Several things turned me around, but prayer was the main thing. When I finally began to pray about it, I really prayed—not just muttering something now and again. Several times a day I was on my knees, more or less begging for help. I know now that the Lord doesn't turn you away when your prayers are sincere like that."

More or less begging? Several times a day? "Wow," Kristy thought. "That would be like saying I can't make it without the Lord's help. And I can't. That's what I have to do."

It is what any of us have to do when temptation is strong. When we are finally humble—"more or less begging"—the Lord joins forces with us against our enemy—temptation.

In the promise we have quoted, Alma mentions prayer and one other thing—watching. In another place, he says it again: "Be watchful unto prayer continually, that ye may not be led away by the temptations of the devil."[1]

A watchful driver is always looking ahead on the road, always checking the rearview mirrors, always studying the car just ahead. A batter has to focus on nothing but the baseball. A receiver has to watch the football into his hands. A good mother knows what her baby is doing all the time. The lifeguard has to constantly scan everyone in the water. Watching avoids failure, avoids disaster.

Kristy found that she had to monitor her thoughts, watch out for those feelings and mental statements that start the cycle of depression, and start a new pattern of thought immediately. Brother Bennett probably had to combine his prayer with vigilance. He had to keep a sharp eye out for upcoming temptation, like the watchful motorcyclist who sees the oil spill way ahead and drives around it.

Watching allows us to do our part. It allows us to drive around, to avoid every possible temptation. By prayer we ask the Almighty to do his part when the challenge is still too great for us.

Jesus commanded emphatically, "Ye must watch and pray always, lest ye be tempted by the devil."[2] Without these twin acts of faith, we have no promise.

44.
HE LOVES ALL HIS CHILDREN EVERYWHERE

God is mindful of every people, whatsoever land they may be in; yea, he numbereth his people, and his bowels of mercy are over all the earth. Now this is my joy, and my great thanksgiving; yea, and I will give thanks unto my God forever. (Alma 26:37.)

The offer of salvation is broadcast by stages. Not everyone knows just yet, but every last one is on the schedule. The last one to hear is just as sure to be invited and encouraged as the ones who have already been contacted. A great surprise awaits those who haven't yet opened their invitations.

The offer will be made to everyone we see on the freeway or at the market or on TV or at large gatherings, and to everyone we can't see and can't imagine. Our Father doesn't have special mercies for his favorite children and lesser mercies for his regular children. He doesn't have any regular children. "All are alike unto God."[1]

He had each one in mind when planning out the difficult and generous offering of Christ—"prepared from the foundation of the world for all mankind."[2]

The Atonement is a bridge that gets everyone home. We descend into mortal life and need a way back. The bridge came of enormous forethought and expense. The Designer and Builder had it all figured out before any of us left home. The way back is reliable or else he would not risk sending us away. Everyone ever born in any day will eventually be guided to that bridge.[3]

"I remember that thou hast said that thou hast loved the world, even unto the laying down of thy life for the world."[4]

If only each of us could begin to see how he feels about the others of us.

Not sensing how good our Father is, some don't think there is much difference between his self and our selves. It is so important and so startling to sense his goodness, that King Benjamin described it as being "awakened."[5]

In the culture where Mei was raised, the idea of a personal God was not approved. But when she studied anatomy in school, Mei felt there was a God who had made her. She learned about the intricate passages that supply blood to her eyes, the dozens of lacey muscles that control the direction and focus of her eyes, and the incredible process of gathering light and sending signals to the brain and interpreting them as beautiful images. She was awakening. Her eyes were being opened.

Mei heard of people who believe in a loving God, and she secretly agreed with them. The evidence continues to pour in, and it is more than belief. She knows that the One who created her loves her personally. It is too real to be imaginary. Someday, Mei will learn of the plan designed for her return home. She will be further awakened. Like billions of others of every nation, she will see the bridge and gladly cross it.

"Who can say too much of his great power, and of his mercy, and of his long-suffering towards the children of men?"[6]

45.
TEACHERS WITH A FAMILIAR VOICE

The Lord doth grant unto all nations, of their own nation and tongue, to teach his word, yea, in wisdom, all that he seeth fit that they should have. (Alma 29:8.)

Long ago we lived with a quiet, piercing voice that could always be trusted.[1] We miss it. We grasp now and then at voices we hear, hoping we have found that one again. We are usually disappointed. We don't go along with the disappointing ones. We wait for the real thing.[2]

What makes the voices of inspired teachers so familiar and genuine? For one thing, the voice of God's quiet Spirit attends their voices. For another thing, you can trust these teachers, much as our Father can be trusted.[3]

They are doers. Their honesty and hard work makes it possible for us to open up a spot in the heart for their words to take root. When a talker speaks it is one thing; when a doer speaks it is another.

As Alma gave advice to the next prophet, Helaman, he focused on the matter of teaching. What was Helaman to do for the people? "Teach them to humble themselves. . . . Teach them to withstand every temptation. . . . Teach them to never be weary of good works." He wasn't just to jabber about these things.

Helaman's job was to help the people desire them, and to help them know how to do them.[4]

Suppose I had been hired to teach people to do math, or teach them to cook meals. Suppose I got up and said, "Okay, now. You people sit down at these desks and do some arithmetic. If you are discouraged, don't worry. I'll be back again tomorrow, and once again I will tell you to sit down and do some arithmetic. Good-bye." What good would that do?

What if I said to someone who had never tasted good cooking and had rarely even seen it, "All right now, just go ahead and cook. Come on, come on, get on with it. Cook." Shame on me. That isn't teaching. That isn't even good nagging.

The gospel teacher has a bigger job than uttering certain words about righteousness. She or he is a living and attractive illustration who has given effort to the price and challenge and timing and manner and joy of righteousness. As we get familiar with the goodly life that attends the teacher's words, we are automatically becoming acquainted with the living Being who sent the teacher to us.[5]

The Lord prefers our teachers to be familiar with us and familiar to us—to know our society because they grew up in it, speaking our language in our way. There are fewer steps from where we are to where our Lord is if his representatives are not aliens.

He doesn't care to have glorious strangers show up and shake the earth under our feet. The promise is that his messengers will be down-to-earth. They will be approachable, with modest and honest voices, easy to trust—reminding us of him.

46.
A HARD PAVED ROAD

Because ye are compelled to be humble blessed are ye; for a man sometimes, if he is compelled to be humble, seeketh repentance; and now surely, whosoever repenteth shall find mercy; and he that findeth mercy and endureth to the end the same shall be saved. . . . Yea, he that truly humbleth himself, and repenteth of his sins, and endureth to the end, the same shall be blessed—yea, much more blessed than they who are compelled to be humble. (Alma 32:13, 15.)

Humility is a wonderful frame of mind. It sees and admits the truth.

A farmer loves the soil when it is humble—soft, loamy, ready, willing, cooperative. The coach loves the athlete who is like that—hard-working, able to see the need for improvement. The parent appreciates the obedient child—soft-hearted, cheerful. The teacher looks forward to the open, absorbent, attentive student.

When a favored team loses unexpectedly, the coach may find them willing to work harder in practice the next week. The rambunctious child who doesn't feel very well has a softer voice and is more submissive to the caring parent. The arrogant student may need a taste of failure before being willing to be taught.

This mortal world is famous in eternity for its abundance of losses, illnesses, and poor grades. We would not wish them on anyone, but one of the reasons we are here is to have these things. Sometimes, they are what we need. Humility makes a human being beautiful, whether the beauty was self-induced or imposed by hard circumstances.

If we could visit the spirit world and interview the Zoramites who lived out their proud and blind lives centuries ago, they might tell us that they wish they had been humble when Alma came to them. "If only we had been downtrodden—like the folks we once ridiculed—we would not have been so smug, we would not have rejected the truth."[1]

Without humility, it is nearly impossible to see things as they really are, so a certain man named Nehor easily deceived the proud and prosperous people of Ammonihah. His exciting ideas left most of the people unable to believe a prophet.[2] A year after Alma's arrival, the fortunes of that blind people had reversed. Every soul that had rejected Alma's message was dead. The city was desolate, unlivable, filled with the corpses of Alma's critics. In the spirit world, those people probably wished something had been done, before it was too late, to humble them. So much for the ideas of Nehor.

Two little boys were playing in the nice, soft sand. They wanted to drive their toy cars over to the castle. "But it's too squishy. We need something hard," one of them said. And they went in search of rocks and boards.

A family drove as far as they could up the mountain, but the road ended part way. "Oh good," said a daughter, "we get to drive in soft stuff now." But it wasn't good. They could go no higher without a hard road.

Soft is not so good when you are trying to make a journey. Humility is like smooth pavement that opens the way upward. But smooth also means hard. Hard experience can make the way clear, reveal the laws, pack down the squishy pride, open the eyes. It can make the road smoother and make us better travelers.[3]

47.
GROWING YOUR TREE

If ye will awake and arouse your faculties, even to an experiment upon my words, . . . if it be a true seed, or a good seed, . . . ye will begin to say within yourselves—It must needs be that this is a good seed, or that the word is good, for it beginneth to enlarge my soul; yea, it beginneth to enlighten my understanding, yea, it beginneth to be delicious to me. (Alma 32:27–28.)

Most people would think that if you stay out of trouble and if you have fun, you will harvest a great life. But when Alma tells us how to grow a great life, he insists on very different "ifs": One is that you have to plant the "true seed." Another is that you have to conduct the experiment fully "awake" with all your "faculties."

Maybe we could illustrate the need for the true seed by telling about a man who did everything he could to raise great corn, except that he planted rocks, just to save money on seed. And we could tell of his neighbor, who did slightly better by planting cactus seeds. But there is no such story. Nothing that stupid has ever been done.

Or has it? Maybe some of us have tried to reap the harvest Alma promised—an enlarged soul, an enlightened understanding, and a delicious taste—by planting something besides the one and only seed that can do the job.

A seed is something like a composer who merges single notes together into something grand and magical, or an artist who draws from separate tubes of paint to make a canvas into a world we may visit and never forget. A shriveled little speck of gray or brown organizes sleeping materials into something that lives and grows, something beautiful and majestic, thousands of times bigger than the seed that began it, and it makes a thousand more seeds while at it.

To an untrained eye that doesn't know about seeds, "the word" might seem unpromising, like a speck of gray or brown. Of course, if we don't work, the seed shrivels whether it is good or not. One of the saddest plots in history is when people don't cultivate the good seeds they have planted. (Unfortunately, something that stupid really has happened before.) But if we will work, a new life begins. It has those three features Alma listed.

We know our soul is enlarging because we can discern between good and evil, make decisions, resist temptations, and get along with others in ways that were too demanding before. The experiment is producing strength.

We know our understanding is being enlightened because old questions are being answered, and we sense our Father's view of things as he teaches us. The experiment is producing understanding.

We know that the seed produces something delicious because we can already taste it. It is satisfying. The experiment is producing joy.

We are not guessing at any of these results. They are all there, they are all absolutely good, and they are all absolutely real.[1] Something inside us knows that "every seed bringeth forth unto its own likeness."[2] That is, good can come only from a good source. We'd better stick with this experiment. It will only get better.

48.
THE GREATER MERCY

Yea, thou art merciful unto thy children when they cry unto thee, to be heard of thee and not of men, and thou wilt hear them. (Alma 33:8.)

Now and then you hear of someone being honored for their seventy-fifth wedding anniversary. That is a long time, at least for marriage in this world.

But when do we hear of a couple being honored for being 100 percent happy? For having harmony every day? For having a relationship of constant trust? For being close to the Lord? Or useful to him?

Well, who could measure such a thing? What news organization would care? It wouldn't be anyone's business anyway. And that is just the point. The question of a close and happy relationship would be the business of that couple and their God, and very few others. It might even interfere with the relationship to bring the public into it.

What we know of a married couple—what we see in public—is the tiniest fraction of what they share. We hardly know them at all. They share daily prayers and dental bills, flu germs and family decisions, births of children and deaths of relatives. Private matters are important to the bond.

Scientists often find that as soon as they try to study some natural condition, the condition isn't natural anymore. Using a nuclear microscope alters the atomic particles. The natural behavior of a child can change when an adult walks into the room, especially if that adult is Mom.

The personal relationship we have with our Father in Heaven is the most natural condition in the universe. But privacy is crucial. Without this, the bond is disturbed.

Nephi's relationship with the Lord is mostly hidden to us. For eight years he traveled in the wilderness, but what are we told of revelations or insights during that time? What tender mercies were granted in those 3,000 days? We know little about it. That is between Nephi and his God. The privacy is part of their bond.

A married couple can best trust each other and give private mercies to each other when they are perfectly sincere, never showing off to the world. And nobody needs to know how much we do for God, or every detail of his constant care.

Our connection with the heavens is delicate. We know the scratchy sound of a radio that isn't tuned. Perhaps we also know what happens when we are pretending to be tuned to the heavens but are scanning for other signals at the same time.

Fortunately, there are no Spirituality Sweepstakes, no Closeness to the Heavens Contests, no Testimony Trophies or Prayer Championships. Our Father appreciates the way we pray and think to be heard only by him, the way we serve and live to be seen only by him. It is the token of friendship. That opens the gates of total trust. It justifies his greatest mercies.

49.

PROSPERING IS A SIMPLE MATTER

*My son, give ear to my words;
for I swear unto you, that inasmuch as ye shall keep the commandments of God ye shall
prosper in the land. (Alma
36:1.)*

Dear Son,

"You asked how I like having all the things I use in my work. You're right, a person would have to be pretty rich to own all this stuff. Of course, none of it is mine. The army owns it all, and they trust us with those aircraft you looked up on the internet, and all the other equipment and facilities we use, and our impressive headquarters, just so we can serve. Our job in airborne support is to take care of a lot of people. Besides protecting them from the enemy, we take in all kinds of supplies, and sometimes run rescue missions.

"When I wake up each day, I'm not thinking about how much fun I'm going to have using these things. Instead, I think about the people who depend on me. And I'll tell you what, little buddy: Flying a plane is fine, but the purpose of the plane is the great thing. I'm glad to be a pilot, but I'm really lucky to have an important job."

To prosper is to succeed. But to succeed at what? Some purpose, some mission.

For the disciples of Christ, the

mission can be demanding. We have people to care for. We protect them, we bring spiritual and temporal supplies to them, and we often rescue them. In all cases, the mission calls for faith and worthiness.

But it helps to have an orderly and peaceful headquarters, such as a meetinghouse or a safe place to live. We may not need a cargo plane, but we may need a way of getting around so that we can actually be in the presence of the people we serve, and so that we can keep our appointments with the Lord and with his people. We may need a place to study, access to knowledge, presentable clothing, and the ingredients of health. Depending on our stage in life, our culture, and our calling, the list will vary.

To prosper is to succeed at our mission. The historic old promise is that if "ye shall keep the commandments of God ye shall prosper." Time and again it has been spoken and proven.[1]

We will have the tools we need. Those who are worthy to serve will have what it takes to serve. They may not have the health or the wealth to fill someone else's role, but they will be equipped for their own.

It's just "stuff," and not even our stuff. The great thing is that we have a work to do.

You or I might have introduced the promise by saying, "As far as I can tell . . ." or "They say . . ." or "Evidently, there is reason to believe . . ." But Alma said, "Give ear to my words; for I swear unto you . . ." Those are words to be sure of, the words of solemn testimony.

50.
THE ONGOING DRAMA OF THE BOOK

He promised unto them that he would preserve these things for a wise purpose in him, that he might show forth his power unto future generations. (Alma 37:18.)

Great stories, the kind that grip us, are about purpose. The ancients knew that a gripping story was unfolding in those shining plates. They didn't know the purpose in detail, but they were satisfied that it was "known unto God."[1] How could they have known details, way back then? There would be too many reversals, too many writers, kindreds, migrations, wars, and miracles yet to surface.

Even today, the great drama is still too young to grasp. There are still too many events yet ahead, too many nations yet to be wrapped in the arms of the book, too many lives yet to be renewed, too many miracles still needed to carry out the wise purpose.

The book is a marvelous work of stories. We can think of it as a pyramid of dramas.

At the base of the pyramid is the epoch we find in the book itself. It tells of the founding of new nations out of refugee families, of the ministries of prophets, and of the national suicide that comes by ignoring truth. Because this founding story is absolutely true, the other stories in the pyramid can be trusted.

Next is the story of the book's coming forth. It is the saga of a metal record asleep in the ground forty generations, of a young seer who gets the record after seven years of waiting, and who even then is badgered by enemies insane with hate. The translation is a miracle at every phrase, made possible by discernment rarely known even among the prophets. The story of the prophet who translated the book is as real as the stories of the prophets who wrote it.

Upon the coming forth is built the next layer of truth: the going forth. There are many honest hearts on this earth, and as the book goes forth it wins these hearts by power. It was designed to satisfy righteous hunger in any person of any race. It is now read in a hundred languages and will be read in a hundred more. The book will thrill hearts in every village of the earth.[2]

At the summit of this pyramid of purposes is the story that the book creates in every life that sups from it each day. God's purpose was not simply to make nations, to make a translation, or even to make a best-seller. His purpose was to fill his children with power. What happened anciently when only part of the book was used for teaching? The sanctifying of "many thousands of the Lamanites." What will happen in our day when all of the book is used in teaching? The Lord will "show forth his power" to sanctify more of his children.[3] But not only Lamanites, and not only thousands.

What else would we expect from the greatest author in the universe?

51.
THE BIG SECRET ABOUT LOVE

See that ye bridle all your passions, that ye may be filled with love. (Alma 38:12.)

The promise, as always, is rooted in a principle. The fruit of the principle seems almost too good to be true—"filled with love." But we can see that the principle is true.

We can think about the most perfect and loving persons we know. There is an ever-present temperance and modesty, like a harness that directs their powers. We can think of Jesus himself. He is a limitless lodestar of love because he is a Son of unswerving obedience.[1] We can think of the Heavenly Parent, who was the first to love us perfectly, from whom we inherit every commandment and every passion.

Horses are not interested in the shiny machines that drive near their pastures. They would rather find another blade of grass than consider a passing truck. But if they did look up and give it some thought, one horse might say to another, "Look at all the alfalfa that truck is hauling. Why, the hay is still green and heavy. There must be tons there."

"Yes, I can see that. I wonder how many of us it would take to pull that much weight."

"Hundreds. Like, enough horses to pull 50 stagecoaches, or to make a stampede that would cover this whole valley with a cloud of dust."

"Wow. A real thundering herd, all packed into one truck. What's the secret? How do they do that anyway?"

"I hear they blow up the fuel in a way that captures the power. They actually make these terrible explosions inside the engine, like a thousand little blasts of dynamite going off every minute. The secret is that it's all controlled and timed. Instead of blowing the truck to smithereens, the force is channeled so it makes the wheels turn."

"Reminds me of when the boss puts a bridle on me and gets all these big muscles of mine to do his work for him. By the way, in my opinion you're a very smart horse."

"Yes, I am. But all this thinking makes me hungry. Let's eat."

For just two horsepower, that was a pretty good conversation. But they missed something more powerful. In the cab of the truck there is a man and his wife. The man is driving, and the woman is sitting close at his side. They are happy and in love.

They are talking together about the big life they share. They are discussing everything from the price of alfalfa to the upcoming marriage of their daughter. They have combined all their powers of spirit and feeling and body and mind into one life. If they weren't polite and kind to each other, if they were slaves to their powers and passions, if they just came, went, ate, spoke, spent, thought, or acted without a bridle, their life would be blown to smithereens. It would not be a life of meaning and beauty, filled with love.

52.
THE VITAL "SPACE" BEYOND DEATH

There must needs be a space betwixt the time of death and the time of the resurrection. . . . The spirits of those who are righteous are received into a state of happiness, which is called paradise, a state of rest, a state of peace, where they shall rest from all their troubles and from all care, and sorrow. (Alma 40:6, 12.)

Now and then we feel a need for "space." In the great plan, two "spaces" are absolutely crucial. One is the space between pre-existence and resurrection, a time of repentance and refinement, the space between two heavens.[1] It is like the long space between the beginning of school and the end, just long enough to finish the course.

The other is the time between physical death and resurrection. It is set within the other space, toward the end. It is a time to finish homework, to take care of last details before the course is over.[2]

Each year after the Indianapolis 500 racing event, an awards banquet is held. Drivers and mechanics and owners come in elegant clothing to dine together, to be honored, and to make little speeches. Is the banquet held right after the race? No. After a few hours? No. Later that evening? No. After the final weeks of intensity and the final days of preparation around the clock, every one needs a space of time to recover. So the banquet is held the day after the race. Even then, some are too spent to attend.

After a footrace like the Boston Marathon, you would be lucky to get the runners to attend anything, anytime soon. They need a space of time to rebuild tissues and energy. Even their minds are worn down from the physical struggle.

Speaking of minds, something similar happens at the end of college final exams. Don't expect the frazzled and sleepy students to show up for a day or two.

But death can be even more exhausting than these other events. Yes, the spirit is freed from its tired body. But this race was the real race, the endurance race that drew on every reserve. This exam was the ultimate, draining test.

For the righteous who have just died, the small space before resurrection is a "state of rest." After all, most death occurs in great difficulty—after prolonged disease or a violent accident. Some have just been dispatched by an enemy or suffered a natural disaster. The event that brought death may have been unexpected, unfair, even unbelievable. Suddenly, one is cut off from familiar routines and places, and from beloved people.

It takes time to set trauma and drama behind, to sort it out and leave it alone, turn to new projects and learn new joys. Spiritual recuperation is a re-gathering of perspective, learning what the lessons were all about, getting the big picture that was so elusive before, getting answers to old questions.

Alma also calls the little space "a state of happiness." Of course. Happiness is the purpose of existence.[3] The righteous are ready for it in a fullness they could not taste while running a race or taking a test. There is no reason to postpone peace and contentment any longer. Paradise isn't just a place but also a space of time before the awards are given. And then comes eternity.

53.
THE GLORIOUS RESURRECTION

The soul shall be restored to the body, and the body to the soul; yea, and every limb and joint shall be restored to its body; yea, even a hair of the head shall not be lost; but all things shall be restored to their proper and perfect frame. . . . And then shall the righteous shine forth in the kingdom of God. (Alma 40:23, 25.)

Hector made a sparse living running the old spindle shop left behind by his father. There, in the highlands of Chile, he shaped wooden pieces for a local furniture factory. The rickety lathe on which he did this work had to be turned by his helper, who would peddle on a bicycle frame connected to the machine. Through the generosity of friends, Hector obtained a loan and bought a big modern lathe for his shop. As he began each working day, he could hardly contain his joy in using such a durable, elegant, powerful tool.

We are promised a perfect body, upgraded and powerful. And it will be beautiful.

To the poor, nice clothing is almost magical—the fit, the fabric, the dignity. To see oneself in a fitting-room mirror, dignified and beautiful, is a pleasant shock: "I am of the same race as respectable people! Look at me."[1]

The promised resurrection will be upgrading and beautifying. It will also be a liberation.

"Brothers and Sisters," the branch president was saying, "let this glove represent the physical body, and my hand will be the spirit within." He held up the empty glove so all could see. "My hand is the spirit before birth. And this," he said as he put the glove on, "is the spirit clothed in a body after birth.

"See what gives personality to the glove? The hand inside. If you take the hand out of the glove," and he dropped the empty glove to the podium, "the hand goes on living."[2]

"Now, because this is Marva's funeral, I'm adding something else to this lesson." The branch president put the glove back on and began wrapping it in rubber bands. "As you know, Marva lived inside a disabled body. She could hardly move, but there was something lively inside, looking at you out of those shiny little eyes. She was trapped in there, the way my hand is trapped in this glove." He held up his hand, bound in rubber bands.

"But now what happened? Her spirit is free!" He quickly removed the glove and held up the liberated hand, moving his fingers. "She's free," he said again. "And when she gets a perfect body in the resurrection, she will still be free." He put the glove back on, this time without the rubber bands. He kept stretching and moving his fingers. "She will never be trapped again. Free forever."

To be upgraded and beautified and liberated will be wondrous. But to rise out of our sins will be even more wondrous. We will leave behind clothing that is not only old and ill-fitting but also soiled and ill-smelling. The Redeemer relieves us of our worn outer garments and, if we let him, redeems us from the odious inner lining as well.

What will it feel like? We'll be finding out in a moment not far off, and a moment more real than any we have ever had.

54.
THE TRUE FAITH AND THE TRUE CHURCH

Now ye see that this is the true faith of God; yea, ye see that God will support, and keep, and preserve us, so long as we are faithful unto him, and unto our faith, and our religion. (Alma 44:4.)

Having the true faith is different from having something similar to the true faith, or a faith we think is true or wish was true. If we are true to something untrue, that is one thing. If we are true to the truth, that is very, very different.

Little Lori tries to do wonderful things. She can't read yet, but she surely wants to. If you hear her somewhere in the house, telling a grand story in a swelling voice, you can bet she has a book in her hands. Of course, it may be upside down.

Lori has her parents trained to put a little strip of yellow tape on the end of any stick she brings in the house. That makes it into a "cando," which she can use to guide you through the dark. That's all very fine, during the daytime. She sincerely wants to guide you safely. But after the sun goes down, don't follow this girl.

In the latter days, the actual truth will come to people who only thought they had the truth. They will notice the difference. "They shall know that it is a blessing unto them from the hand of God; and their scales of darkness shall begin to fall from their eyes."[1] They will see, and see brightly.

110

If Lori offers you a plate of "newtishus" food, be warned. The little round things aren't peas but lumps of dough with green food coloring. The long things aren't green beans. If the chocolate cookies look a little like mud cakes, eat at your own risk. This girl wants to make you healthy. That counts for something. Thank her. Honor her. But don't partake.

Partaking of the real truth is not only safe but also nutritious. Those who once ailed from poor "newtishun" will partake of the real thing and "become a delightsome people."[2]

Lori has thought up some ways to survive in outer space. You wear some full-bodied pajamas (complete with feet, of course), her mother's gardening gloves, and her brother's football helmet. She means you no harm. But if you stepped into outer space under those conditions, you wouldn't live long enough to freeze to death.

In the time of King Benjamin, people were surrounded by various religious systems, each offering the conditions needed for salvation. After he presented the true religion of Christ to his countrymen, Benjamin warned, "There is none other salvation save this which hath been spoken of; neither are there any conditions whereby man can be saved except the conditions which I have told you."[3]

They say you can't march to more than one drummer. Likewise, we can hearken to only one voice at a time. All of us choose the voice we will follow.[4]

You can probably imagine Lori's map "from the Sapific Ocean to the Fancy Home," whatever that is. There are a lot of well-meaning maps. Only one will get us Home.

55.
DISABLING THE DEVIL

Yea, verily, verily I say unto you, if all men had been, and were, and ever would be, like unto Moroni, behold, the very powers of hell would have been shaken forever; yea, the devil would never have power over the hearts of the children of men. (Alma 48:17.)

Eventually, people like Moroni will shake the powers of hell forever.[1] But all men aren't like him just yet. If he couldn't shake those powers forever all by himself, why did he even try? Because he could shake some of the powers of hell. He could shake them for a while.

Just one of his efforts postponed the violence for "the space of four years."[2] In that space, the devil was disabled. It wasn't forever, but four years is something. Some souls were saved in that time, some families were formed, some folks finished their mortal probation. Some good was done that could never be undone. To bless for only a while is worth it.

While Amalickiah (who reminds us of the devil) was creating as much hatred and unrest as he could, Moroni (who reminds us of Christ) was working hard for harmony and freedom.[3] The hard work and generous intentions tell us something about being "like unto Moroni." But there is more.

Moroni knew that the war against evil is a war of "preparations." The description of Moroni's campaign uses the word several times.[4] Satan wins when we battle him carelessly, casually. After long experience, Moroni warned us not to "sit still" and think that "because of the goodness of God ye could do nothing and he would deliver you."[5] The massive fortifications around Nephite cities were enormously expensive. But Moroni made no apologies.[6]

People "like unto Moroni" know that we cannot win against evil if we imitate evil. That is, we cannot afford to argue, accuse, and criticize among ourselves. It was Moroni's "first care to put an end to such contentions and dissensions among the people; for behold, this had been hitherto a cause of all their destruction."[7]

Moroni could win against evil because he wasn't diseased with jealousy or shrunken by pettiness. Instead, his "heart did swell with thanksgiving to his God, for the many privileges and blessings which he bestowed upon his people."[8]

He was physically strong, but that has nothing to do with the battle against Satan. Moroni was a giant because he was "firm in the faith of Christ."[9] His leadership was not about physique or technique. In dark times, it never is. Leadership is about character. We oppose the devil by being unlike him.

Character distinguishes Moroni from Satan. It makes him superior to Satan. Satan is small, driven to madness by those who are prepared, firm, and faithful. They remind him of the heaven he once rejected and continues to hate. He cannot touch them. He shakes before them, as do his powers.[10]

"Let us labor diligently; . . . for we have a labor to perform whilst in this tabernacle of clay, that we may conquer the enemy of all righteousness."[11]

56.
THE WORD AND OUR RETURN HOME

Whosoever will may lay hold upon the word of God, which is quick and powerful, which shall divide asunder all the cunning and the snares and the wiles of the devil, and lead the man of Christ in a strait and narrow course. . . . and land their souls, yea, their immortal souls, at the right hand of God in the kingdom of heaven, to sit down with Abraham, and Isaac, and with Jacob, and with all our holy fathers, to go no more out. (Helaman 3:29–30.)

It will be unspeakably nice to someday "sit down" with our God and our noble ancestors. We will have to avoid "snares" (deadly nooses) and "wiles" (insidious tricks) Satan has set for us. The promise is that we can get around all that.

In the verse just before the promise, Mormon says "the gate of heaven is open unto all." Whoever really wants to go Home and sit down is free to do it. The privilege will be granted to "whosoever will"—the person who really seeks it. If what? If we "lay hold upon the word of God."

"He imparteth his word by angels unto men, yea, . . . women also. . . . Little children do have words given unto them many times."[1] We can only imagine the experiences that showed this principle to Alma over the years.

The sweetness of sacred truth comes from prophets, from scripture, and in the hour of prayer. But the taste is sometimes there in the presence of friends, young and old. In various ways, the quiet angels call our attention to the pure and stirring truth we need.

Larry lived in a sparsely populated

part of Canada. The burning question in his life was how to find a marriage companion. The question was linked to others, such as schooling and career. But Larry had this faith: If you think it through and look at all the angles, and if you ask for and live for and watch for the Lord's messages, the direction will come.

One morning, Larry was focused on 3 Nephi 20:18, about the gathering of Israel. Other questions were set aside, for Larry knew that scripture study was a time to leave the alleys of mortality and visit the halls of eternity. He was noticing that the Lord gathers people in natural stages.

Suddenly, his mind was filled with the answer to his dilemma. He should aim for the profession he wanted most—teaching math. He should apply to a certain university. In the process, he would find his companion. A decade and a half later, Larry is teaching math at a junior college. He has a wife and children to sit down with him someday in the presence of God. He still stays close to "the word," watching for messages that will guide his life.

Man-made literature, no matter how appealing, has no such power.[2]

When "the word" comes, our job is to "lay hold" on it. Imagine edging along a high ledge. Suppose there is a railing, and you only lightly touch it with a finger as you lose your balance. Suppose you only look at it as you tumble over the ledge. No, we are to reach out with vigor, bring our hand down on the railing with a wallop, and grip it with whitened knuckles. When the word comes, we take it firmly, stick to it, and follow it Home.

57.
THE ONE SAFE SPOT

It is upon the rock of our Redeemer, who is Christ, the Son of God, that ye must build your foundation; that when the devil shall send forth his mighty winds, yea, his shafts in the whirlwind, yea, when all his hail and his mighty storm shall beat upon you, it shall have no power over you to drag you down. (Helaman 5:12.)

Here, the Lord guarantees that a storm will come. The storm will beat upon the house. No insurance policy can prevent the flooding torrent and buffeting wind. The wise man plans on the storm. He knows how to build a life, but he also knows where to build it.

We don't have to worry about the house but only about where we will put it.

What does it mean to build upon the rock of our Redeemer? It is to translate his revelations and commandments into daily events and cycles. His insurance is in force only if we make real payments. To merely say we are going to do it, or to sincerely admire the rock, doesn't seal our house to it.[1] Some policies do nothing until all is lost. But his is a guarantee against the loss itself. And it is not for a mere house but for a home, a life.

We stopped at the simple dwelling where the branch president lived. By some fortune we found the whole family there. Gentle respect—akin to reverence—swept over us on entering their tiny place. The children were bright, they were beautiful in spirit, they were radiant. The Church had been established in this land for a generation or so. Before us stood the fruits, a family that had grown up unto the Lord.[2]

We might be tempted to imagine another family, a family surrounded with just about every physical advantage known to modern man—life in a gated community, a home decked out with electronic security and all the media, cuisine meals, and modern vehicles. But there is little peace in that house, for the foundation is man-made. If a storm comes, the peace is gone in sixty seconds.

In the scene before us, we beheld a life absent of insurance or hospitals, doorlocks, exercise equipment, central heating, appliances, even shoes. But it was also absent of contention, confusion about what is important, discouragement, and darkness.

If I had to choose, in which home would I want to be raised? Which home would I choose for my child? Which is safest? The home that is most "blessed," even if least equipped. The one where my children would "know to what source they may look" for peace.[3]

Wouldn't I prefer for my children a home like the 2,000 sterling mothers kept?[4] Those women trusted the promises as we would trust a mass of deep bedrock. In their common, motherly tasks, they made sure to reconnect their homes to the rock every day.

Let the lightning terrorize the sky and rattle the earth. Let hail slash the hillsides, and the rivers rise. The rock of a faithful life cannot move, doesn't even vibrate a little. It is unfazed, solid, poised, and safe.

58.
HANDS THAT CAN SEAL

Behold, I give unto you power,
that whatsoever ye shall seal on
earth shall be sealed in heaven;
and whatsoever ye shall loose on
earth shall be loosed in heaven;
and thus shall ye have power
among this people. (Helaman
10:7.)

The false religions that flourished among Book of Mormon peoples took their buildings very seriously.[1] After you build something of stone, you can admire it for hours, all with the thought that it can never go away. But all ancient stone buildings, anywhere on earth, go by this one name: "ruins."

In Mayan ruins, tree seeds got into the narrow joints and grew into forest giants, rending the walls to rubble. Earthquakes shifted whole villages off their foundations. Massive vines scrambled stone blocks the size of railroad cars. Volcanic lava now encases cities. Declarations of proud kings and false priests, carved into rock to last forever, are but shallow, unreadable depressions full of moss and lichen.

Something that will survive ten centuries is pretty impressive until nine centuries, 99 years, 11 months, 29 days and 23 hours have passed. At that point, it is like something built to last an hour. Anything that doesn't last forever is useless for almost all of eternity.

But among some of those ancient people, once in a great while, came someone who could make things last forever. The power to make something last on and on—eternity upon eternity—can be entrusted only to a prophet who is faithful and true in all things. Nephi, son of Helaman, was one of these.

To this man of nonstop maturity and unrelenting best effort, the Lord said, "I will bless thee forever; and I will make thee mighty in word and in deed."[2] Into his trusted hands was placed the highest of God's rights, the right to seal something off from all death, to seal it up to the endless eons.

Nephi traveled the land often enough to see the pompous stone corridors and palaces. He knew that these shapes of rock— soft enough to be altered by the puny tools of man—were doomed to oblivion. He didn't offer to make them eternal. But he could seal covenants and people and relationships.

One of the most terrible penalties ever pronounced is this: "The places of your dwellings shall become desolate."[3] Oh, the unspeakable calamity—and how unnecessary—when a family loses its future, when a home is dispelled, becoming empty and hopeless. No wonder a certain number of Nephites, on hearing that such a possibility hung over their heads—and knowing that it had already been visited upon some of their friends—"began to weep and howl."[4]

How sad for us if no man such as Nephi walked among us. But heaven be thanked that in a church that gathers the nobles of heaven, there walks a noble of the nobles, one whose perfectly trusted hands are clothed with power to make earthly connections endure—one to whom the Lord has said, "Thus shall ye have power among this people." We have such a man, and we are such a people.

59.
THE UNFETTERED OFFERING

If ye shall come unto me, or shall desire to come unto me, and rememberest that thy brother hath aught against thee—Go thy way unto thy brother, and first be reconciled to thy brother, and then come unto me with full purpose of heart, and I will receive you. (3 Nephi 12:23–24.)

Suppose a neighbor comes to your door with a large basket of food. You can see a carton of milk and a loaf of bread peeking over the rim. There is cheese and fruit down inside. "I wanted to share this with you," he announces.

You are just going to invite him in when another person approaches. The stranger says to your neighbor, "Hey, you didn't even pay for that." Taking the bread from the basket, he goes away in a huff.

Your neighbor says, a bit sheepishly, "Sorry about that. But there is still all this other food I'd like to share with you, so please accept it as a gift." But now another stranger shows up, grabs the fruit, and yells, "How dare you pick fruit from my trees without even asking!" The gift basket is getting lighter.

Before your neighbor can start again to declare his generosity, the local grocer arrives on the scene, pointing his finger at your neighbor. "I finally caught up with you, you thief. If you ever come into my store again, I'll have you arrested." The grocer takes the milk and cheese and goes away.

"Well, I don't suppose we'll be bothered again," your neighbor says, peering into the basket, "because there's nothing left in here. I really wanted to give you something, so please accept this empty basket as a gift from me to you." You take the "gift" and thank your neighbor, who hurriedly leaves. That's when you notice that this basket is the very one that was taken from your back porch the week before.

The Lord wants to "receive" us, of course. But what we present to him—our heart, our life—should be clear and free, not full of debts we owe to others. Fettered gifts, all tangled up with other people's claims and complaints, are not gifts at all.[1]

This is a principle of harmony. To ignore everyone else as I approach the Lord is like randomly tapping the keys of a piano. It is not music. It is not harmony. It is jarring noise. The Lord doesn't demand a masterpiece, but he insists on a life of harmony.

Most of our siblings in this dark world are struggling. Perhaps they are easily offended because of a heart full of scars. The reason is probably not our business.[2] Our business is to avoid being that way ourselves, and to ease the problem for them if we can. When they are offended at "aught"—anything at all, including innocent mistakes—we can go to them and seek harmony. We can apologize, express respect, offer the hand of friendship, try to avoid further offense. Then we can go to the great Redeemer and offer an unfettered heart.

60.
THE GROWN-UP CHILD OF GOD

Love your enemies, bless them that curse you, do good to them that hate you, and pray for them who despitefully use you and persecute you; that ye may be the children of your Father who is in heaven; for he maketh his sun to rise on the evil and on the good. (3 Nephi 12:44–45.)

A good man holds up a squirming infant and says, "This is my son." It is technically true. A few decades later, the same man points at a grown and goodly person and says, "This is my son." There is now more meaning in what the father is saying.

If we resemble our Father, we are more than offspring. We are growing up—a convincing likeness, children who are like the Parent. There is a striking resemblance in our manner, in our hopes, in the way we conduct ourselves. Someone might come up and say, "Pardon me, but you remind me of God. Is he your father?"

A certain learned widow had spent her life teaching in the school of her little town. Her life's dream was to found a library that would enrich knowledge for all the citizens. To this end, she collected thousands of books over the years. After she died, her two daughters were left to decide what should be done with all those books.

"They are valuable," said the younger. "We can sell them and make a fortune."

"No," said the older, "that was not our mother's dream."

"Then let us divide them between us and have them in our homes for our own children."

The older sister answered again, "We should not do that either. We know what our mother intended for these books. Let us put them in the school. Then they can be studied by our children and also everyone else." The older sister was more grown-up. She had adopted her mother's wish as her own.

Our Father freely shares his belongings. They are not ours but his. He creates them and governs them and maintains them only in order to share them. It is one thing to let him be our provider, to accept his gifts and enjoy them. It is another to join him in this enterprise, to be instruments of his generosity. At some point in growing up, we wish to be his partners.[1]

Of course, he shares much more than material things with us. If he "has caused that [our] hearts should be filled with joy," that can be shared too.[2] Like books or money or knowledge or hope or time or testimony, joy is a "substance" that could "perish" with the person who only hoards it.[3]

Beyond the principle of fairness, there is also a principle of generosity.[4] Fairness says the owner may keep what is his. Generosity says the owner may also share what is his. What is his to keep is his to give away. This is the mature kind of love. Those who are blessed are free to bless.

That is the way of God's grown-up children.

61.
HEAVEN HONORS A QUIET DEVOTION

When thou doest alms let not thy left hand know what thy right hand doeth; that thine alms may be in secret; and thy Father who seeth in secret, himself shall reward thee openly.
(3 Nephi 13:3–4.)

Wilbur's run for student body president was the biggest popularity contest he could imagine. He had never liked the principal but now made sure to call out to him in the hallways when other students were around. "Hello, Mr. Jensen. How's everything going in the office?" Mr. Jensen would only smile and walk on.

One afternoon, while Wilbur and his friends were putting up a "Vote Wilbur" banner, Mr. Jensen came and quietly said, "Wilbur, can I talk to you in my office?"

In the office, Wilbur sat down and eyed Mr. Jensen. "Well, what do you want?"

"Oh, I thought I might tell you how everything's going in the office," the principal smiled. "You're interested, aren't you?"

"Look," Wilbur said, "I don't want to be rude, but I've got to get back to my sign."

"All right," Mr. Jensen sighed. "I'll tell you what's on my mind, Wilbur. I want a good relationship with every student, and certainly the student body president. But I wonder if you have any idea how miserable the school year would be for both of us if it's not really friendly—you know, if you're just trying to impress people."

From the impatience on Wilbur's face, Mr. Jensen knew he would have to say this another way. "Would you like to know why I'm the principal here?" he asked. That sounded pretty interesting to Wilbur, so he nodded.

The principal continued. "I guess I'm in this position because I like to help people, and I never worry about who gets the credit. You know, Wilbur, it's the one who succeeds in private that ends up succeeding in public." As the young man thought about this, Mr. Jensen added, "You know who I hope will win the election? Not necessarily the one who greets me in the hall, believe it or not, but the one who talks to me in private."

There are two worlds in our relationship with God: the private one and the public one. We can't want both at the same time. We may end up with both, but only if we seek the first. Oddly, if it is the public one we seek, we will end up with neither.

Only the private connection with him is worthy of our focus. If we train both eyes upon it as if they were one eye, we will have all the light we can bear. To focus anywhere else leaves us in the dark.[1]

One way private devotion appears openly is by the way it engraves itself in the face—not forced there by God, not painted on or acted out. It is engraved from within. The image of God distills as the owner of the face consents to it in private decisions and desires.[2] It begins in the mind and proceeds to the surface.

The Lord is never ashamed of his real friends. He honors them first privately and then "openly."[3]

62.
THE GENEROSITY OF GOD

Ask, and it shall be given unto you; seek, and ye shall find; knock, and it shall be opened unto you. For every one that asketh, receiveth; and he that seeketh, findeth; and to him that knocketh, it shall be opened. (3 Nephi 14:7–8.)

I'd like a hat," someone said. The clerk looked up and saw a young lady at the counter.

"Good," the clerk answered. "We have plenty. I'm sure you'll find one you like."

"It needs to fit my head. And look good on me, and go with the clothes I have at home."

"That's for sure," the clerk agreed. "Go ahead and look around. Try on any you like."

The young lady didn't move. "Can't you just go pick one out?" she asked.

"Well, if this hat is for you . . ." the clerk began. The young lady's brow wrinkled a little. The clerk patiently went on, "If it's for you, you'd better see if it fits your own head, and see how it looks on you, and decide how it would go with your clothes. We find that no one can try on a hat for another person."

We can't wear a hat without a head. There can't be an answer without a question. Could there be "answers" in the back of a math book without any problems in the front? There must be a question.

126

And, generous as our Father is, he cannot do the asking and seeking for us. The one with the need is the one who has to try on the answer, just as the one with the hunger is the one who has to eat.

But once the question is asked or the request is made, and once we actually exert ourselves to go looking and trying things on, he answers. He doesn't hide from our requests. He isn't like that. He is generous.[1] He asks us to ask. It is a command. He isn't reluctant to answer. Answering is what he does. He is the Great Answerer in the universe, "quick to hear the cries of his people and to answer their prayers."[2]

But if he is generous and sees our need, why pray? Isn't He always aware, always watching? Yes, but when we pray, something wonderful happens.

Something wonderful happens when a baby begins to smile and coo. The connecting of eyes, the response to the parent's voice, the sweet effort to speak—these put the relationship on a new level. Prayer connects us to him who wishes to be more than a guardian. He seeks the bond of friendship.[3]

When we open the conversation, when we invite him to us and plead for His attention, he is no longer waiting for personal contact between himself and his child. When we break the silence, the contact has begun.

By prayer we speak through a thin curtain. We aren't talking to a mere clerk in heaven but the most wonderful being in the galaxies. Through the curtain he hears, and the promise is that "it shall be opened."

63.
A Sign of Real Goodness

Do men gather grapes of thorns, or figs of thistles? Even so every good tree bringeth forth good fruit. . . . A good tree cannot bring forth evil fruit, neither a corrupt tree bring forth good fruit. (3 Nephi 14:16–18.)

Wouldn't it be terrible if some people were just bad, and there was simply nothing that could be done about it? Is that how it is? Are some people good to the core, unable to be bad, while others are like permanently corrupt trees that can bring forth nothing but evil?

The Lord has never taught such a thing. What he has taught, instead, is that we can change. If we have been acting like one kind of tree, we can change to another kind. We can look for a way—his way—to change the very heart of the tree so that it can bear a new kind of fruit. We can avoid the life of a thistle. We can cease to produce thorns. We can become completely different to the core.

This is clear not only in the words of Jesus but also in his work. In his grove, the hearts of the trees can be changed.

King Lamoni is a corrupt tree when we first meet him. This man thought nothing of having his servants put to death if they didn't prove athletic enough to defend his animals.

"What? You let someone steal one of my animals? Off with your head!" Or something like that.[1]

This corrupt tree changed. He had to believe the gospel. He had to let go of every conflicting thing he could. He begged for change.[2] Lamoni brought forth all the good fruit he could, and the Lord intervened at the core of the tree.[3] The same with Lamoni's wife, Lamoni's parents, Lamoni's people. The change was for them as it always is: the Lord's favorite fruit—obedience—began to appear.

Some people find it hard to pay tithing at first. Such fruit has never grown there before. But as they do it anyway, the heart of the tree changes. The tithing becomes automatic. It just shows up in season, almost without effort. The same is true of getting to a meeting the Lord has called right in the middle of a day off.[4] Or avoiding coarse language. Or having family prayer. What seemed unnatural to begin with becomes simple, consistent, and pleasant.

Even the tiniest good fruits tell us that something good is going on in the tree.

A woman complained to her marriage counselor, "My husband is so fake sometimes. But I know what he's really like. I see his bad side."

This statement didn't seem quite right to the counselor. Finally he asked. "I wonder if it's possible that his good side is just as real as the bad side, maybe even more real." She hadn't thought of it that way.

But that is the promise. If you can bring forth good fruit, it isn't fake. It's real. You can keep it up. You can cultivate that side until the whole tree is good all the time.

64.
FULFILLING THE LAW TOGETHER

I am he that gave the law . . . ;
the law in me is fulfilled. . . . As
many as have not been fulfilled
in me, verily I say unto you,
shall all be fulfilled. . . . Behold,
I am the law, and the light.
Look unto me, and endure to
the end, and ye shall live; for
unto him that endureth to the
end will I give eternal life.
(3 Nephi 15:5–6, 9.)

In the realm of man's law, there are two sides. On one side, the legislators and judges and enforcement agencies make the laws work. On the other side, everyone is expected to abide those laws. Both sides are necessary and good.

In the realm of God's law, there are two similar sides. On one side, there are divine plans and projects and prices. We don't understand that side. We know it is difficult. We know that making the laws work calls for an infinite, heroic effort from the Father and the Son. Because they do their part, the laws are perfect and bring perfect results.

On our side of God's law, there are commandments, ordinances, and principles. Fortunately, our price is considered enough even though it isn't infinite.

When we live our side of the law, it puts Christ at the center of our feelings and thoughts. That had to be achieved in a special way before Jesus came to earth. Remembering him was even more difficult then than it is now. People were not able to simply look back in history to think of him.

They couldn't study eyewitness accounts of his miracles or suffering or resurrection. There was no vast selection of story and art on the subject.

And yet that former system worked. We know this from something written by Jacob, son of Lehi, who lived hundreds of years before Christ. He wanted his descendants to know "that we knew of Christ, and we had a hope of his glory many hundred years before his coming. . . . And for this intent we keep the law of Moses, it pointing our souls to him."[1]

The format of the law is different now, but the purpose is exactly the same, "pointing our souls to him." It does this in several ways. It gives us constant reminders of him, it teaches us what kind of being he is, it trains us to be like him, and it gives us a way to show our love for him.

Whether we are speaking of the law before his atonement was performed or the law that was given after, it is fair to say that he is the law. In fact, that is just what he said in the promise we have quoted. He is the law because he made it, he met it and mastered it.

On his side, the law is about us. On our side, the law is about him.

His part took sheer endurance at certain points. We know that the last hours and final split seconds of his life were a steep hill for him as he chipped away at his ominous mission. He did the whole infinite list, task upon task. He asks that we too endure, though our list is small. In a sense, we and he are partners, each enduring in our own way, on our respective sides of the holy law, fulfilling it together.

65.
HIS EYE IS ALWAYS ON ISRAEL

I will show unto thee, O house of Israel, that the Gentiles shall not have power over you; but I will remember my covenant unto you, O house of Israel, and ye shall come unto the knowledge of the fulness of my gospel.
(3 Nephi 16:12.)

Over a million railroad cars travel the railways of the United States. Yet, few are lost. Regular humans—people who can think of just one thing at a time, aided by brainless computers—manage these hunks of steel that all look about the same. Humans track every route and repair, every product and passenger.

We each have about a trillion neuron cells in our brains. These are intricately managed, along with thousands of little signals stuttering back and forth per second. Images, patterns, and memories are stored by the millions. If we get bumped on the head, the data may be jumbled a while. But in time the brain can reorganize itself, and we start remembering and thinking again. We do all this without knowing how we do it.

We might consider libraries or license plates or national debts, but the point is: If mortals can do all this, then God—who can concentrate on an unlimited number of things all at once—can certainly keep track of his children.

And he isn't just a tracker and manager. He cares about the whole story of humankind and at the same time each human story. He is a part of each story and always will be.

The lonely railroad cars we see on sidetracks near the highways, or sitting on little spurs of track in the industrial parts of a city, seem lost forever. But each one is known. Each one has a history, each one cost much to build and is valued by its owner. Each one has a future we could not imagine by looking at it. Such is the case with each child of God, whether part of the house of Israel or not. Each one is somewhere at this very moment. The Father can tell exactly where, and just what lies ahead.

To us, world history might look like a wild disaster. The nations seem doomed to perpetual war, confusion, and decline. But all this was foreseen. God is only using the disasters as refining fires.[1]

The lost are never, never forgotten. He has a plan for each return—a plan that was formed long before it was needed. Past upon past piles up, the generations fall asleep without a visible hope. The chosen people, and all other people, dwindle in unbelief, poverty, bondage, and near extinction. But they "shall not be forgotten."[2] We must not fret. Our faith in the promises leaves no place for a sense of doom.[3]

If the past was being watched, so is the present. So is the future. The promise that blessed us will bless our children with the mercies and friendship of God. "As many things as have been prophesied concerning us down to this day have been fulfilled, and as many as go beyond this day must surely come to pass."[4]

66.
ALL MAY JOIN THE CHOSEN FAMILY

If the Gentiles will repent and return unto me, saith the Father, behold they shall be numbered among my people, O house of Israel. (3 Nephi 16:13.)

There is such a thing as adding a remarkable ingredient to food that is already very good. They say that adding an herb called cilantro to salsa and other Mexican foods really makes a difference. If that isn't a very convincing example, how about adding steak to macaroni and cheese? In any case, the Gentiles are an addition like that. They are not obvious members of the race of Israel. And yet, they make a big difference.

The people of Zarahemla were royalty, heirs of the Jewish kings. When another ethnic group came among them—Mosiah and his Nephite friends—the Zarahemlans could have rejected the migrant newcomers.

Fortunately, they welcomed Mosiah and made him their king. This one decision led to their advancement as a culture, their national survival, their conversion to the gospel, and their political freedom.[1] That story reminds us of how some of the latter-day Gentiles have not only joined the covenant of Israel but have also become Israelites in every sense. They are blessing and gathering the chosen seed.

Twenty-six hundred years ago Nephi prophesied that "the Lord God will raise up a mighty nation among the Gentiles." It would be a redemptive nation.[2] It would also be a very privileged nation, "nursing" fathers and mothers to a forlorn mankind.[3]

God would enrich them—"lifted up by the power of God above all other nations"—so that he could enlist them. Their wealth would be more than temporal. He promised, "I will bring forth unto them, in mine own power, much of my gospel." That gospel knowledge would make them extremely useful to mankind.[4]

What a story. People once scorned by Israel, the enemies and even the oppressors of Israel, will become saviors to Israel. They will be equipped for this service by reading an old book written by Israelite grandfathers, long-since dead. "Those who shall be destroyed shall speak unto them . . . [as it were] out of the ground."[5]

There was once a large family with numerous problems. The family had managed not to split up, but the home was a constant scene of contention. One member of the family, a daughter named Margaret, was active in the Church.

The daughter married a choice man named John. At first, the family thought John was a bit odd, like Margaret—happy, peaceful, and close to the Lord. But in time the parents accepted him as a son. The children saw him as a hero. Everyone in the family felt close to him. Over the years, John influenced many wonderful changes in that clan.

"I, Nephi, would not suffer that ye should suppose that ye are more righteous than the Gentiles shall be."[6] The Gentiles will rank among the most righteous people who ever lived, a gem of the ages.

67.

A Solemn Testimony to Our Father

This shall ye do in remembrance of my body, which I have shown unto you. And it shall be a testimony unto the Father that ye do always remember me. And if ye do always remember me ye shall have my Spirit to be with you. (3 Nephi 18:7.)

Now dear, you're not going to forget, are you?"

"Of course not. Would I forget?"

"Okay, then. Be sure to turn it off at five o'clock."

"Turn what off?"

"The oven!"

"What about the oven?"

"What do you mean, 'What about the oven?'"

"Just kidding."

"It isn't funny."

Sometimes, forgetting isn't so funny. It ruins dinners, gets people lost, causes accidents. It can lose a soul. Our "testimony unto the Father" every seventh day is that we will not forget. We will remember what was important to us when we were thinking clearly. We will remember what we promised. We will remember the past and the future.

How can we remember all that? A string on our finger? A rock under our pillow? The prophets recommend another approach: "Enter into a covenant with him. . . . Whosoever doeth this, and keepeth the commandments of God from thenceforth, the same will remember. . . ."[1]

The mortal mind slips. But we can keep the vital things in it if we follow the gospel program—renew and obey. Renew the covenant over and over, and during the times in between just keep obeying. This allows even the weakest to keep a grip on eternity.

The tokens are simple—a sip of water and a morsel of food. The words of the prayer are understandable. The ceremony is held at a time and place we can count on. It is easy enough to present our testimony unto the Father. We just have to show up.

In rare cases, showing up is impossible. But generally, the sacrament is a statement anyone can make, a statement unto the Father regarding his Son. If we keep showing up, if we commemorate him week after week, we are saying that we have not dwindled in unbelief and ingratitude.

Why not just make the covenant once and be done with it? That would be a little like saying, "Oh, I heard beautiful music one time. I've seen a sunset, I have looked at my child. Once was enough. I talked with my friend once. I took a bath three years ago. I ate a meal back in '94. That was enough, thanks." Logic like that is a bit crazy. It lacks heart and mind. We are drawn to the sacrament by love and by deep, recurring need.

The water of baptism is a space between two lives, the old and the new. Sacrament meeting is a space between two weeks, the old and the new. Sacrament meeting is a gate to heaven, open every week. It is a stepping-stool to the next level, the beginning of a better chapter. It is a table where we exchange gifts with the Lord, where we promise to remember him and he promises to walk with us.

68.
A SPECIAL KIND OF PRAYER

Whatsoever ye shall ask the Father in my name, which is right, believing that ye shall receive, behold it shall be given unto you. Pray in your families unto the Father, always in my name, that your wives and your children may be blessed.
(3 Nephi 18:20–21.)

Kevin is a pretty normal ten-year-old. That's why it came to pass that he was eating a few extra cookies for a treat during a ward activity. And because they were "extra," he was eating them all alone out in the meetinghouse foyer. And that is why his mother wasn't on hand to remind him to put the dental retainer back into his mouth after eating the cookies, which is why the retainer got left behind on a little table when the family went home that evening.

Those retainers are expensive, so the family came back that very night to look for it. But it was not on the little table anymore (though cookies crumbs could be seen in the area). It was not on the floor or in the lost and found. Kevin and his family made it a matter of prayer that night and several times the next day. They decided they had to go back and try again. They had another prayer and returned a second time to the meetinghouse.

They looked in all the same places, and in every room and hallway. The time came to either give up or pray again. They were alone in the building now, so they knelt together in the foyer—Mom, Dad, Kevin, his little sister, and his two little brothers. After the prayer, it was very quiet, and then Mom said, "We haven't been looking high enough."

"High enough?" Dad asked, and he gave a perplexed glance at the ceiling.

Mom nodded confidently. "Have Kevin stand on your shoulders. Then go around the building looking up high." So they did that, and as they got to one of the light fixtures along the ceiling, there was that little retainer. How did it get there? Well, there were other little boys at the ward activity that night; we'll just have to guess.

Heavenly Father never loses track of anything, not even little things in light fixtures. He can see what we are missing. He can let us know when we should look higher.

He is pleased by family prayers. And when the request is for something "which is right," that is a powerful combination. What could be righter than a blessing upon a family?

If we pray with our families, we will have such experiences now and then—answers that are sometimes specific, blessings that are especially gracious, the occasional spiritual outpouring. These memories build up over time, like courses of stone in a castle wall, like layers of metal upon our shields.

Perhaps the most lasting and valuable and life-changing gift we can give a child is the tradition of praying morning and night to the Father, in the name of Christ, with the whole family. It is a commandment from Jesus himself. And the promise is that husbands and wives and children will be "blessed."

69.
INVITING, INCLUDING, AND SAVING

If he repent not he shall not be numbered among my people. . . . Nevertheless, ye shall not cast him out of your synagogues, or your places of worship, for unto such shall ye continue to minister; for ye know not but what they will return and repent, and come unto me with full purpose of heart, and I shall heal them; and ye shall be the means of bringing salvation unto them. (3 Nephi 18:31–32.)

Tara walked with eyes fixed on the back door, hardly noticing her grandpa as she passed. "You look pretty serious there, young lady," he said.

She stopped. "I have to do something really sad," she said.

"Does it have something to do with that doll in your hand?"

"Yes. I have to throw her away." With head lowered and eyes just ready to overflow, she held out a small rag doll. "She's dead," Tara explained.

"Really?" Grandpa held out his hand. "Can you show me the cause of death?"

The doll had suffered at the teeth of the family cat. It was a gruesome sight. Both eyes and an arm were missing. "Do you remember the story I told you about when my buddy was hurt in the war?" Grandpa asked.

"Sure. You found him all bloody. He didn't move or anything," Tara recalled.

"Exactly. We thought he was dead at first. But he wasn't, was he?"

Tara remembered more of the story now. "You said that . . . if you just left him there, he would have died. But you spent all day helping him, and he got better."

Tara watched as Grandpa slowly turned his attention to the doll. "Have you got a little time right now?" he asked. She nodded. "Good," he said, "'cause that's what we'll need so we can do the same thing with your doll that we did with my buddy."

They found some buttons and made new eyes. They took the arm away from the cat and sewed it back on. When they finished, and Tara was admiring her renewed little friend, Grandpa said, "Don't ever give up on someone you love, Tara. It might seem like they're done for. But they'll probably make it if you just spend some time with 'em."

Our instructions from the Lord are to never, never cast someone off. If a person's name is removed from the records of the Church, that isn't the end. It isn't the final judgment. It may even be a beginning. In a redemptive work, we keep making beginnings.

Nephi noticed a big theme in the writings of Isaiah: Hope. He suggested that we study those words, "that ye may have hope as well as your brethren . . . ; for after this manner has the prophet written."[1] After that manner—the giving of hope—have the prophets written and spoken. The message of heaven to earth is hope.

But we can't give much hope unless we spend some time. When the eyes and limbs are injured, someone needs to be there, giving time and hope—being a friend. This calls to mind the prophet Mormon, a perfect friend: "Notwithstanding their wickedness I had led them many times to battle, and had loved them, according to the love of God which was in me, with all my heart."[2]

70.
IMITATING HEAVEN

I give you these commandments
because of the disputations
which have been among you.
And blessed are ye if ye have no
disputations among you.
(3 Nephi 18:34.)

It is hard to misinterpret what Jesus said here. As usual, or even more than usual, his language is crisp and clear: No disputations. "No" means none. Not even a few disputes, not even little ones. Either I have no disputation in my heart, in my home, in my words and weaker moments, or I have not yet overcome the tendency.

To illustrate that there are no exceptions, he once used the example of doctrinal dispute. "Neither shall there be disputations among you concerning the points of my doctrine."[1] So, none of that either. If we should not argue out the truths of salvation, we should not battle over the lesser things either.

Isn't it okay to defend our views or our dignity? It is one thing to say what we believe kindly and briefly when we have the permission of our hearers—and to say it only once. But the spirit of contention never leaves it at that.[2] We can go without an opinion, or let others have theirs, rather than stir up ill will.

A child may fuss or cry in sacrament meeting. That is the way with children. But it is a different kind of cry when they hear their parents argue. We can get all sorts of illnesses in this world. But there is a different kind of sick we feel at the sound of anger.

In the paradise of righteous spirits, perhaps not everyone is perfect yet, and not everyone knows all truth. But it is free of contention. To be a place of peace, it would have to be a place of patience. To be a realm of rest, it must be a realm of respect. It is that way all the time there.[3] It is also that way in certain homes.

Among the evil ones on the other side, there is no end of dispute. It doesn't matter if both parties are wrong, or even if both are right. There will be a fight. There will be scorn. Scorn is a sign of something deadly going on in the heart.[4] It tells us that a force opposite to heaven has found a way in. Scorn is our imitation of hell.

Even truth can get us in trouble. Some "truth" is poorly timed, or doesn't matter. Some facts are not edifying, cause no rejoicing, create no real understanding.

If we "settle this once and for all," will it settle anyone? Will it even settle me? Will my good reasoning throw a feeling of peace over the relationship?

Some of us think we can have inner peace if things are peaceful on the exterior. But we are wrong. It works the other way around. Only peace on the inside—with no argument with God and with no mischief in our hearts—guarantees against dispute. We won't correct or retaliate or rage. We will be blessed with our own heaven wherever we go.

71.

A Steady People in the Latter Days

It shall come to pass that I will establish my people, O house of Israel. (3 Nephi 20:21.)

To "establish" is to make stable, steady, immovable, certain. In the few words of this promise, a world of certainty is offered to us in an uncertain and unstable world.

It isn't just something that happens. The Lord is personally involved. He says, "I will gather my people together. . . . I will consecrate their gain. . . . I am he who doeth it. . . . I will establish my people."[1] It is his idea, his project, his covenant. He cannot be distracted from it.

If a ship is built on good principles, it will keep a steady course on open seas, even in a storm. Passengers will go up on the deck for hours and marvel as the ship cuts through the vast unsettled surface around it. But if the laws of ship-building are ignored, the vessel shifts on the giant swells and trembles under the violent winds.

If society abandons eternal laws, confusion and destruction rule. At the same time, Zion will keep plowing her smooth path.[2]

There was a time under the leadership of Alma the Younger when the Church was surrounded by degradation and hostility. But in the Church itself, there was modesty, equality, and pure truth.[3] The members were steady in their homes.[4] They were an island of peace in an angry and tossing ocean.

This same blessing is promised to us, for "every dwelling-place of mount Zion. . . . A shadow in the daytime from the heat, and for a place of refuge, and a covert from storm and from rain."[5]

Unfortunately, the refuge is needed. There are latter-day storms. The sea around the Church will not always be smooth. The Lord speaks of a "consumption decreed"—a time of decline and loss. But as the consumption spreads in the world, a harvest of goodness will "overflow" in the Church. Those who pass this time with integrity will be more confident and powerful—they will be established.[6]

How can we be steadfast if we never face a contrary wind? The storms will prompt the faithful to deepen their keels. In the troubled earth, the Lord's people will have a different experience from the rest of mankind—an untroubled experience.[7] "They shall obtain gladness and joy; sorrow and mourning shall flee away."[8]

Soon after his conversion, Amulek found himself teaching a hostile audience. He was offered a chance to avoid violence and at the same time to get a lot of money—something equivalent to thirty thousand dollars—if he would simply speak a few words denying his testimony. How did he react? He did not pause or tremble. He was established, like a great ship cutting through the ocean waves as if they were not even there.[9]

72.

FOR THE CHILDREN OF THE PROPHETS

Ye are the children of the prophets; and ye are of the house of Israel; and ye are of the covenant which the Father made with your fathers, saying unto Abraham: And in thy seed shall all the kindreds of the earth be blessed. The Father having raised me up unto you first, and sent me to bless you in turning away every one of you from his iniquities; and this because ye are the children of the covenant. (3 Nephi 20:25–26.)

The Savior is going to bless everyone eventually, but of course he has to start somewhere. Who should be the pioneers of his blessings? Who should be the first ones to be turned away from their iniquities? His plan is to begin with the modern-day offspring of ancient prophets.

If we were going to recruit students for a college, we might start with children of the alumni. If we were trying to get donations to restore an old ghost town, we might start with descendants of its former inhabitants. If we wanted to spread the use of another language, we could begin with the children of those who spoke it. They know the basics, and they have the traditions.

Besides, the Lord promised the prophets he would stay in touch with their children. To keep his promise to the ancient ones, and as a good way to approach all mankind, he is starting with a certain family, the family that was long ago appointed to bless mankind.

Before the children of the covenant can be very useful, they have to be turned away from their iniquities. Alma the Younger was such a one. Enos was such a one. The sons of Mosiah were children of a prophet.

We see the Savior of children at work during his visit to the Nephites. Several sacred stages led up to the point when angels would minister to the children. It seems to be the confirming event, a sanctifying experience that prepared those children to be the greatest society in ancient American history. Perhaps a ministry to the children of the faithful was on the Lord's agenda all along.[1]

Could it be that the marvelous era of peace was made possible when parents saw their children bathed in light and surrounded by heavenly friends? Were the angels imparting a new measure of faith to those children? Might it be that some of the angels were ancestors of the Nephite families gathered there? Is this a glimpse of some wonderful pattern going on more often than we know among faithful families?

King Mosiah earnestly sought some reassurance about his sons. In answer, he got the highest assurance possible: "Many shall believe on their words, and they shall have eternal life."[2] Yes, his sons would have eternal life. But so also would the people his sons would reach. The children of this prophet would not only be saved, but they would also go a step further. They take up the cause of their parent. They would know the joy of the prophets.

The Messiah was raised up to save the children of the prophets, the children of the covenant. And they are raised up to help him save the others.

73.
A HOLY DESTINY FOR THE JEWS

Then will the Father gather them together again, and give unto them Jerusalem for the land of their inheritance. Then shall they break forth into joy— Sing together, ye waste places of Jerusalem; for the Father hath comforted his people, he hath redeemed Jerusalem. . . . Put on thy beautiful garments, O Jerusalem, the holy city, for henceforth there shall no more come into thee the uncircumcised and the unclean. (3 Nephi 20:33–34, 36.)

Just as Moroni prayed for the descendants of people trying to kill him, Jesus is going to draw into the circle of his blessings that lineage whose fathers crucified him.[1] The children of the assassins will gather to the Messiah.[2]

But these are not just children of assassins. No, that is perhaps the least important thing we might say about the Jews. They are children of faithful martyrs like Isaiah and Jeremiah, Zenock and Zenos. They are refugees from the holy stories of ancient history. They are charter members of the anointed, royal family. They were writers of the holy word, preservers and defenders of the holy truth, and perhaps preservers of mankind itself, for thousands of years. They are cousins to the Son of God, members of a redemptive race.

Yes, certain generations of this family would "turn their hearts aside, rejecting signs and wonders, and the power and glory of the God of Israel." Yes, a branch of their clan would "wander in the flesh, and perish, and become a hiss and a byword, and be hated among all nations."[3]

But their family will make the

148

greatest comeback in history. And then their holy kinsman, the Holy One of Israel, will "remember the covenants which he made to their fathers." And they will not only return to the real estate, but they will also come Home.[4]

The Jews will resettle their old land. It will be "restored," and so will they. Their home will be made new, and so will they. Jerusalem and its surrounding land will be a splendid and holy home again, even holier that it was before.[5]

The "captive daughter" will become a queen. The city of dust and rubble, of anxious eyes and roiling crowds and tortured prayer calls, will become bright and kind, quiet and united. No wicked or divisive person will be found there, no explosives, no retaliations. Jerusalem will be wholesome and holy and happy.[6]

We cannot comprehend the past sorrows of the Jewish people. There is no earthly history of their trauma, for such a story is beyond the scope of human words. The words "victim" and "martyr" and "hero" are too understandable. The ideas of "disappointment" and "homelessness" and "injustice" are too sterile to match the human realities that waged on for centuries. Nor are we able to quite foresee the adventures that still await them. But they have a holy destination. That we know. It is sure.

"Then shall the offering of Judah and Jerusalem be pleasant unto the Lord, as in the days of old, and as in former years."[7]

We pray that the long and troubled story will soon reach its glorious conclusion.

74.
A
Marvelous
Work to Do

In that day, for my sake shall the Father work a work, which shall be a great and a marvelous work among them. (3 Nephi 21:9–10.)

Brother Pollard was leaving the meetinghouse when a tall, elderly man approached him. "May I ask a question . . . Mr. Pollard I believe?"

"Of course. You're the man visiting the Colton family. Am I right?"

"Yes. Dr. Colton's the name," the man explained. "I was in your class today, and I have a question." Brother Pollard nodded, and the man continued, "Did I hear you refer to your Church as a marvelous work?" Brother Pollard nodded again. "But wouldn't that refer to something rather big and impressive? I've been many places in the world. There are such a lot of people. I've decided that any religion worth anything is going to have to reach mankind, not just their little group. Do you have an answer for that?"

"I believe I do," Brother Pollard answered. "But, I would rather show you than tell you. If you're free tomorrow, I'd like to take you for a little drive." A time was set, and the next day they drove to the Church Distribution Center in Salt Lake City. On the way, Brother Pollard outlined some of the "marvelous" events that are scheduled to take place in the latter days: growing in all the nations, a Zion here, a Jerusalem over there, temples everywhere, members everywhere.[1]

By the time they reached their destination, Dr. Colton was reeling a little. "It sounds like you have your work cut out for you, Mr. Pollard." Brother Pollard nodded and smiled.

On entering the Distribution Center, Dr. Colton had to stop just to let his eyes take in the long walls full of manuals and supplies, the orderly aisles with media and computer software and scriptures. "Your church produces all this?"

"Of course, and in many languages. The real operation is at the Distribution warehouse. But since we can't visit there, I thought you ought to see a little sample." After walking around a bit, they began to exit, and Brother Pollard stopped at a large map of the world. "See the dozens of little lighted dots?" Dr. Colton nodded. Brother Pollard smiled. "Those are where the Church has other Distribution Centers."

As they drove homeward, Dr. Colton was quiet, so Brother Pollard told the story of a prophet named Abinadi. After he was martyred, a small church continued the work he began. It grew and went on to overcome difficulties and do mighty works.[2]

"You might say that's what the Mormons are doing, Dr. Colton. We're continuing the work of a modern prophet, Joseph Smith. He too was martyred, but the work he began is growing in the world. What you saw back there in the Distribution Center is just the beginning. But it has begun."[3]

"I must say," Dr. Colton finally said, "the Church my son and his family have joined is more than I thought it was. It's a marvel."

Brother Pollard smiled. "I couldn't have said it better myself, Dr. Colton."

75.
THE DARK THINGS WILL PASS AWAY

It shall come to pass that all lyings, and deceivings, and envyings, and strifes, and priestcrafts, and whoredoms, shall be done away. (3 Nephi 21:19.)

Mindy had been home from Bolivia just a few days, and she was giving the home evening lesson. "The happiness here is heartbreaking, in a way," she said as she looked around at her family. "You know what I mean? So many have nothing like this."

"But that's why you went on a mission," a teenage brother said, "so they could have it."

"You're right," she answered. "But compared to how many need it . . ." She thought back to an experience she would never forget. "Like, one night, my companion and I missed our bus home and took a shortcut through the edge of the city."

"Uh-oh," Mindy's mother said, already tense. "You mean after dark?"

"Way late, and we'd never been through this area before. We got into this alley-like place, muddy and narrow, strong-smelling. We could hear children crying, and now and then people yelling at each other. We could only imagine what it was like in those little shanties. It was so dark. We were in that alley for just a minute, but I'll never forget it."

The room was quiet as everyone tried to picture the scene. "Later, I tried to imagine how many alleys like that there were in that city. In just that one city, if you spent only a minute visiting each alley and street where there is suffering and poverty, it would take days. So what does our Father in Heaven see throughout the whole world?"

"Just think," Mindy's father's added, "how many places in the world have alleys like that. All the nations. I hear there are a million or so villages and towns just in China alone."

"It's beyond our understanding," Mindy continued. "But what's really wonderful is something else beyond our understanding. The Lord is going to end all this sorrow."

She had her family turn to 2 Nephi 24. "Let's see if I can find it in English . . . Here in verse 3, 'In that day the Lord shall give thee rest, from thy sorrow, and from thy fear, and from the hard bondage wherein thou wast made to serve.'[1]

"I've read that one over and over since we walked through the alley that night. And here's another, in 2 Nephi 21. See verse 4? 'With righteousness shall he judge the poor, and reprove with equity for the meek of the earth.' I found out that judging here means like when a judge or policeman protects the innocent."

"And," Mindy's mother said, "don't think the sorrow is just in the poor areas. Somewhere the Lord promised to remove the adultery and the other terrible things that go on in every income bracket."[2]

"So imagine," Mindy said, "if the wind was howling and then it stopped and everything was totally peaceful. That's how it will be when all the dark things pass away."

76.
A Greater Savior Than We Think

For a small moment have I for-saken thee, but with great mer-cies will I gather thee. In a little wrath I hid my face from thee for a moment, but with everlast-ing kindness will I have mercy on thee, saith the Lord thy Redeemer. (3 Nephi 22:7–8.)

Reality is always surprising. As astronomers learn more about the stars, they aren't bored. They are struck with wonder and sur-prise. As physicists learn more about the smallest particles of matter and energy, they are astonished. There is nothing humdrum about marine biology—it's amazing. We cannot imagine the truth until we see it.

So it is with the mercy of Christ. It is greater than we think, because we can't think of that much mercy. Someday we may, perhaps. For now, we'll just have to believe it is there.

I think I'm gracious if I go easy on my child when he apologizes. Am I gracious if there is no apology? Will I wait while remorse comes slowly? Will I allow repentance to bloom? For a few minutes? A few decades? Centuries? And what if this is someone else's child?

Am I patient if the offender is not a child, is not cute, not innocent, not familiar? What if this is an unsightly, guilty, unfamiliar person who is also violent and insolent? What if the offender harms an inno-cent person? What if that person is my child?

The Surprising Savior keeps his wits and his heart about him under all these circumstances. He keeps reaching for the salvation of every soul—cute or ugly, nice or nasty. Even when he is ignored or defied, he watches for an opportunity to humble and heal the blasphemer or defiant one. Even when his precious followers—and his followers are more precious to him than we think—when they are cheated or insulted or harmed, he keeps a steady course until the great journey for every soul is over.

Not only is the Surprising Savior more patient and merciful than we think; he is also more willing to pay the debts of his foes than we fathom. He has looked into the unpaid bills of the most willful sinners and posted enough to cover them if only they would repent. He hopes they will repent. Is that what we would hope for our enemies?

If I had anything like his power to forgive, and anything like his readiness to pay the debt of an enemy, just how many times would I be willing to forgive and pay, over and over?

And just how many foes am I ready to save? One or two, maybe? Enough to sit around a table? To fill an office? To fill a courtroom? Would I keep forgiving enemies, though they came and came until they filled a stadium? A valley? A world?

Thanks to the Surprising Savior, "they that dwell in the land of the shadow of death, upon them hath the light shined."[1] The people who believed the wrong thing, did the wrong thing, fought the truth, and made his job more sorrowful—does he despise them? No. He is not that small.

77.
TRUE SERVANTS, FUTURE KINGS

They shall be mine, saith the Lord of Hosts, in that day when I make up my jewels; and I will spare them as a man spareth his own son that serveth him. Then shall ye return and discern between the righteous and the wicked, between him that serveth God and him that serveth him not. (3 Nephi 24:17–18.)

Alma, son of Alma, found himself face to face with the armed and deadly Amlici. In the spirit of his offices—as Church leader and as national leader—he uttered a prayer that could only erupt from the heart of a real servant: "O Lord, have mercy and spare my life, that I may be an instrument in thy hands to save and preserve this people."[1] His life was preserved, and he used his days to do what he had been doing all along—to save and preserve his people.

Ammon comes to mind also. His Lamanite friends and converts were not just a quaint project for him. When he arrived in their land, he said, "I desire to dwell among this people for a time; yea, and perhaps until the day I die."[2] He meant it. He was so permanently committed to them that they were known ever after as "the people of Ammon."[3]

Artificial servants—whether slaves or employees or bystanders or leaders—just go through the motions. Real servants—whether they are leaders or bystanders or employees or slaves—do what is needed and do it with heart.[4] In the day when the Lord will "make up [his] jewels" for another chapter of eternity, he will use this standard: "him that serveth God."

In fact, he has been making up his jewels all along. This has been the measure all along. When Alma Sr. was selected as one of those jewels, the Lord said, "Thou art my servant; and I covenant with thee that thou shalt have eternal life."[5] The Lord held Alma close because Alma never held back.

We are reminded of the ancient words, spoken again and again in heaven and earth, spoken in the presence of heavenly hosts and spoken in bishops' offices: "Whom shall I send, and who will go for us? Then I said: Here am I; send me."[6] When we are "sent," we go not as top brass but as servants, on the errand of the One who sends us.[7]

The real servants are the crown jewels—the royalty—of the next world. We can imagine these kings and queens in training. They are gathered to receive instruction and power, making their sacred agreements. They are preparing to be "sent" on their careers of learning and service and proving, perhaps wearing some subtle token to remind them in time to come of who they really are. They go out on errands to "save and preserve" their fellow beings, finding opportunities to draw others into the order of servants.

Kings and queens in eternity are real servants—dressed up in mighty power so they can serve for real and forever.

78.
ELIJAH AND THE HEARTS

I will send you Elijah the prophet before the coming of the great and dreadful day of the Lord; and he shall turn the heart of the fathers to the children, and the heart of the children to their fathers, lest I come and smite the earth with a curse. (3 Nephi 25:5–6.)

The promise is that a heavenly force is available to turn family hearts to each other. Of course, the turning has to happen before the sealing. Would God seal those who are not devoted to each other?

In the first century of Book of Mormon history, Lamanites were already being raised to hate Nephite ways and Nephite religion. But according to the prophet Jacob, something just as dangerous was also developing among the Nephites. He was speaking to the Nephites when he said this about the Lamanites:

"Behold, their husbands love their wives, and their wives love their husbands; and their husbands and their wives love their children; and their unbelief and their hatred towards you is because of the iniquity of their fathers; wherefore, how much better are you than they, in the sight of your great Creator?"[1]

Evidently, Nephite marriages were losing the affection God intends for every couple. Religious people with unhappy homes are no "better" than unbelieving people with unified and loving homes. The Nephites needed that heavenly, turning influence.

158

But it's a big, slow business getting hearts sincerely turned. Our children aren't as simple as we thought they were when we brought them home from the hospital. It doesn't take long for a parent to learn how delicate—and stubborn—little humans can be when you want them to turn in some other direction. It is not like turning an eighteen-wheeler. It's harder.

Human souls are more complex and massive than giant ocean liners, railroad trains, and meteors. Course changes, if they are not to be upsetting, have to be slow and small rather than sudden and severe. A railroad train, if it is to turn around, must leave its present track and go out on a long, slow loop through the surrounding countryside, maybe even disappear over the horizon for a while.

People are like that. They need time for deep change. Without the Living Christ—the attentive and powerful Friend overseeing every family—it couldn't happen.[2] The change would be too mighty. With Christ, it will probably be as his hand works in the natural world: slow and sure, molecule by molecule.

Hearts turned to each other have "accord"—unity. That was vital for the Lehi clan during their travels. "It must needs be that we should be led with one accord into the land of promise."[3] Either they were led forward in unity or not led at all. When a family is in the Lord's hands, there isn't a third alternative.

When King Benjamin's people heard his famous sermon in family groups, and when Jesus sent his hearers home to ponder with their families, this wasn't just an organizational technique or an attempt at crowd control.[4] It was the sacred pattern at work. Families were being turned to Christ and to each other.

79.
A DAY OF GREATER KNOWLEDGE

When they shall have received this, which is expedient that they should have first, to try their faith, and if it shall so be that they shall believe these things then shall the greater things be made manifest unto them. (3 Nephi 26:9.)

The ancient plates were designed to come forth in their entirety—every word, sealed portion and all. But the coming forth was to be in stages. Joseph Smith has given us the first installment. There is more to come. What remains is not an afterthought, a little bonus the Lord hadn't thought of at first. No, the next installment has been planned all along.[1] Like so many things in life, sequence is everything.

Eight-year-old Megan was just leaving the bishop's office when she suddenly remembered something. "Oh, Bishop, I almost forgot," she said. "When you come to my baptism, would you maybe bring my temple recommend with you?" They went back in the office again, this time for a little explanation about how we grow in stages. He told Megan that the temple is something we get ready for, over a period of years. He even said it can be dangerous to do some things too soon.

"When I was young," the bishop said, "I got hired to run a backhoe machine, like the ones you see digging up the street sometimes. I told the boss I could do it, so he gave me the job of

160

pulling the dirt away from a storage shed. I got a little mixed up at one point, and moved a lever the wrong direction. The big old arm of the backhoe went left instead of right—smashed the door right off its hinges. The boss said he was glad I wasn't running the big machine alongside the freeway. 'Out there,' he said, 'a move like that could kill people.' That was my last day on that job!"

For the faithful, the Book of Mormon is only the first installment. For others, it is the last. "If it so be that they will not believe these things, then shall the greater things be withheld from them."[2]

My young son and I were just leaving for the day. We were on a journey to the nation's capital. "Hey son," I said, "let's look at this map of Washington, D.C."

He said, as politely as he could, "Well, Dad, why don't we wait till we get there to look at that map. We're still in Colorado." Good point.

Looking at the map before you are ready for it can be confusing. You wouldn't want to use a map of the last part of your journey to get you through the first part. Evidently, the translation we have so far is for the first part of our journey.

In the next installment, "All things shall be revealed unto the children of men."[3] Then the faithful will know all the things they ever wondered about. And when we know that much, we will approve with more than just a nod of the head. We will fall to our knees in praise.[4]

161

80.
ENSURING A
HOLY
CHURCH

If ye call upon the Father, for the church, if it be in my name the Father will hear you; and if it so be that the church is built upon my gospel then will the Father show forth his own works in it. (3 Nephi 27:9–10.)

In his later years, Hans started reading the Book of Mormon and almost immediately gained a testimony. When he was called to work with the young men in the branch, the list of less-active ones almost overwhelmed him. "It would discourage me," the branch president said to him, "but I remember that this is the Lord's Church, and he will join me in the work. For example," he added with a smile, "he inspired me to call you to help!"

"That's nice," Hans returned. "Can we just sit back and watch the Lord work?"

"No," the branch president answered, more serious now. "The Lord made a true foundation for his Church. But if we don't build on it, nobody will come to live there."

"So how do we build on the true foundation?" Hans asked, looking again at that list.

"Before I got my present calling," the president said, "I didn't notice this as much, but now I see all the time, when I read the Book of Mormon, that the prophets pray about their work. Do you remember reading that?"

Hans thought a moment. "Yes . . . I do remember prophets facing various problems . . . and really praying—even though the Church was true and they were prophets."[1]

"The Lord waits for the prayers of the people, Hans," the president continued, "and when you have a calling, he waits for you to do two things: pray and work. I think sometimes that if our people prayed for the Lord's work more, we would see more miracles in the Church."[2]

"Miracles?" Hans asked. "What do you mean?"

The president pointed at the list of names. "That's what I mean. Do you think you and I can do this?"

To the Savior, his Church isn't just a container of truth. His work is to bring the Father's children back. He has to teach them, cleanse them, perfect them. He has only one Church available for this work, and it must be holy as well as true.

Because the Church is true, we have something to build on. We have things to do with all our might and people to pray for with all our hearts. Even Jesus himself, among the Nephites, prayed unto the Father for them. And then he commanded his people to do the same.[3]

Our job is to help Christ with the teaching, cleansing, and perfecting. It will take miracles. It is a holy task, the work of a God, beyond our powers. No wonder the Father wishes to "show forth his own works" in the Church. If he doesn't, he won't get his children back.

81.
A BOOK THAT PERSUADES THE RIGHT PEOPLE

[The Nephite records] shall go unto the unbelieving of the Jews . . . that they may be persuaded that Jesus is the Christ, the Son of the living God; that the Father may bring about, through his most Beloved, his great and eternal purpose, in restoring the Jews, or all the house of Israel, to the land of their inheritance . . . ; and also that the seed of this people may more fully believe his gospel, which shall go forth unto them from the Gentiles. (Mormon 5:14–15.)

Like a magnet, the Book of Mormon draws certain people out of the neighborhoods of the earth. Whatever the magnetic element is, it stirs the best in these people.

We sometimes recognize some sight or sound or smell from a special moment in our past. As the sweetness comes spilling back, we do all we can to recapture it and re-taste it. It is that way reading the Book of Mormon. It seems almost to whisper, as with a familiar voice, from some forgotten and wondrous chapter of life.[1]

This miraculous process—a filtering, selecting, sifting, and attracting of certain people—was to begin with the Gentiles. Gentile nations have lineages of Israel mixed in, but they are no longer aware of their heritage. They are spiritually asleep. In the latter days, they are very much awake to temporal things and worldly wealth. And when the book comes to them, some of their number— millions of them in fact—awaken. They are attracted to the latter-day kingdom by the familiar, sweet voice of the book.

The promise is that the Gentiles

will carry the book to the Jews and the Lamanites.[2] Jewish hearts and Lamanite hearts discover that same liberating and satisfying power. They know they have found a fountain of truth. Whatever spring brought forth that record can be trusted in all that it produces.[3]

It is pretty easy, in a crowd of people, to get the attention of some and not others, or even to separate the crowd into categories. For example, if you set up a place to get helicopter rides in one area, that would attract some of the crowd. You could get a different group to another area by offering free wheelchair demonstrations. Rap music here versus Bach over there. Nursery rhymes here, hearing aids over there. Bubblegum-flavored ice cream versus spinach soup. And so on.

If there is to be division among mankind—and this is unavoidable—the Book of Mormon helps that division to be along meaningful lines. The "great division among the people" that is to be in our day would not be over who likes spinach and who doesn't, but over who is attracted to the familiar voice in that book and who is not. The book selects those who love to "be persuaded to do good continually," who love to "come unto the fountain of all righteousness," who love the testimony "that the Lord is their Savior and their Redeemer, the Mighty One of Israel," and who love to be taught "the covenants of the Father."[4]

The very people who want to find the Living Christ, live in his way, and do his work are drawn in by his book. It convinces the right people of the right things at the right time.

82.
BEING RAISED TO A GREAT GATHERING

The day soon cometh that your mortal must put on immortality, and these bodies which are now moldering in corruption must soon become incorruptible bodies; and then ye must stand before the judgment-seat of Christ, to be judged according to your works; and if it so be that ye are righteous, then are ye blessed with your fathers who have gone before you. (Mormon 6:21.)

King Benjamin once asked that we "consider on the blessed and happy state of those that keep the commandments of God." That is a fascinating project, but can we imagine being "received into heaven" by the kind hosts who await us? Can we grasp what it will be to "dwell with God in a state of never-ending happiness"?[1] All this is outside our experience. But, we can consider it.

We have seen the relief when loved ones reunite. We can consider a celestial family reunion, "blessed with [our] fathers who have gone before," finding each other perfected, free of flaw.[2]

We know the excitement that attends a conference of the Church, the thrill of expecting the servant of the Lord to come in and to speak. We have seen the rejoicing as believers, who have never met, gather on sacred ground. They are not strangers. They believe the same sacred truths, live the same eternal laws, love the same divine Friend. The bond is immediate and deep. We can consider the feast of friendship and reverence as we someday convene in the presence of the Lord himself.[3]

After dark winter, the shepherd

166

gathers his sheep from a low valley. The weather warms, and he moves them higher. If they follow, they will finally be gathered with him on the mountains in a green and brilliant summer.

After the dark days of Abinadi's martyrdom, Alma went forth gathering. People with a certain hunger "gathered together at the place of Mormon, to hear the words of Alma."[4] They were not hungry for the inspired words alone but were "desirous to come into the fold of God, and to be called his people."[5]

They risked their lives to be in the fold. They pulled up roots and left their homeland, taking only what they could carry. It was the scene of sincerity we can find in every dispensation. No selfish motive, no hidden agenda. They certainly weren't impressing their cynical neighbors. They weren't even trying to impress us. They had no idea their story would be retold. They were gladly paying the price of friendship with their new-found God and his pleasant friends.

To be gathered in this world with the kind and clean, the believing and buoyant, the teachable and trusted—this was worth every earthly trouble to the people of Alma. But there was also the wondrous hope of continuing in this same fold of friends when it convenes in the day of resurrection—abiding with the Shepherd and his faithful sheep forever.[6]

Living happily ever after isn't just the ending for a fairy tale. It is the beginning of a celestial story, the majestic and true story of salvation. "O remember, remember that these things are true."[7]

83.

A World Reserved for the Guiltless

He that is found guiltless before him at the judgment day hath it given unto him to dwell in the presence of God in his kingdom, to sing ceaseless praises with the choirs above, unto the Father, and unto the Son, and unto the Holy Ghost, which are one God, in a state of happiness which hath no end.

(Mormon 7:7.)

One of the first lessons we are taught in the Book of Mormon is that "the guilty taketh the truth to be hard, for it cutteth them to the very center."[1] Laman and Lemuel could see only a part of the truth at that time. It was the hard part, as if they were laying on a bed frame with no mattress.

Later in history, one of their great-grandchildren, King Lamoni, was able to get past the hard part to the broader, fuller truth. He was allowed to see the coming Messiah, to foresee the miraculous birth and the gracious atonement. On merely speaking of this, "his heart was swollen within him." He became so weak by reason of joy that he fell to the earth, "being overpowered by the Spirit."[2]

Was this an overreaction? Was Lamoni's relief and gratitude over the coming Messiah a little overdone? Any reaction, no matter how heartfelt and grateful, would actually be an underreaction, would fail to mirror the full-scale truth. The yawning, moderate interest of the casual worshipper is undersized and naive. Perhaps the underreacting worshiper is, as Lamoni was at one point, asleep.

Lehi was never in greater contact with reality than when he peered into heaven. The scene he witnessed was not what a self-assured, unseeing mortal would expect. Hosts of intelligent and healthy, well-rounded persons were "in the attitude of singing and praising their God."[3]

And countless people across the earth are in brief contact with the truth when they hear or sing Handel's great *Messiah* each year around Christmastime. It is not just a cultural experience. As Lehi noticed, it is an "attitude," a way of feeling about things when we have things straight.[4]

George Handel and all the other composers of sacred music are inspired by heaven to give us a means—a form of expression—that permits pure gratitude and honor to rise from us unrestrained. The static, one-dimensional tones of mere talk are not enough to satisfy this "attitude."

But for such a healthy impulse and indescribable joy, the guilty are not ready just yet. They have other "attitudes" to reckon with first. You can't say "Thank you" very well at the same time you are saying "I'm sorry."

For the guiltless, the presence of God is safe and desirable. It is just the right world for them—just what would satisfy.

The formerly crusty Alma, after finishing up his last painful "I'm sorry," realized that he would never be finished saying "Thank you." For that reason, when he saw the same worshipers Lehi had seen, he exclaimed, "My soul did long to be there."[5] When we no longer need to say "I'm sorry," we will long to be there too.

84.
A BOOK OF VITAL THINGS

If ye believe this ye will know concerning your fathers, and also the marvelous works which were wrought by the power of God among them. And ye will also know that ye are a remnant of the seed of Jacob. . . . And if it so be that ye believe in Christ, and are baptized, first with water, then with fire and with the Holy Ghost, . . . it shall be well with you in the day of judgment. (Mormon 7:9–10.)

I f ye believe this [the Book of Mormon]. . . . it shall be well with you."

In a day when truth is denied—in the prophesied day of doubt—here is a book full of certainty. "It shall come in a day when the power of God shall be denied, and churches become defiled and be lifted up in the pride of their hearts."[1]

After centuries of editing, the book covers only the vital things, the precious, the plain.[2] There is no nonsense here, no glittering frills or silly extras, no pursuit of trivia. It is a book full of vitamins and minerals.

The Lord himself refers to the contents of this book as his "rock." It contains his actual words to the present generation of mankind. It absolutely verifies the truth of the Bible. Joined with the Bible, the Book of Mormon proves the true identity of the Son of God. It makes imperishably clear that we must come unto him in order to fare well in the day of judgment. And it repeatedly tells "all kindreds, tongues, and people" just how to come unto Christ.[3]

Another vital theme in the book is about a special clan of rescuers and nurturers. They are of the original 'House of Israel," appointed to spend their lives blessing all the other "kindreds of the earth." In most cases, these designated drivers for mankind, these carefully equipped workers—"the remnant," as the book calls them—don't even know who they are. The book points them out, awakens them, and fills them with warm conviction about their work. And it shows them, by precept and old family stories, how to go about it.[4]

The book was written by the Spirit of God, it was translated by the Spirit of God, and—wonder of wonders—it is all ready to be read by the Spirit of God. Into the life of an honest reader comes the very power that inspired the writers.[5]

Emerging from this banquet of certainties, this feast of knowing vital things, come those who either partake or refuse. The book has created an era of spiritual insiders and spiritual outsiders, in a way. Those who believe it know the truth. Those who doubt it are left to doubt just about everything else worth knowing.

The records had to survive, "for there are great things written upon them, out of which my people and their brethren shall be judged at the great and last day."[6] Even the day of judgment would be foiled without this book.

If we are to be judged by any book, let it be a plain and kind one. Let us be tested on a book that carries its own power to persuade our minds and change our hearts.

85.
TREATED
LIKE
ROYALTY

Do we not read that God is the same yesterday, today, and forever, and in him there is no variableness neither shadow of changing? . . . But behold, I will show unto you a God of miracles, even the God of Abraham, and the God of Isaac, and the God of Jacob; and it is that same God who created the heavens and the earth, and all things that in them are. (Mormon 9:9, 11.)

If our religious ideas don't include tooth fairies and Easter bunnies, we may consider ourselves pretty grown-up. But if we think that God treated the ancient people like royalty, but would never treat us that way, we have cooked up one of the silliest fairy tales of all.[1]

Our Father was not in adolescence thousands of years ago. He wasn't learning or still working out his approach when he spoke to Adam and Eve or blessed Sarah and Abraham. He is perfect and consistent. He is just as prone to use miracles now as ever.

Mrs. Miller was a single mother living in the poorest part of town. She supported her two little girls on very small wages. After their first discussion with her, the missionaries were impressed with her cheerful attitude. And they were inspired by her immediate faith in the restored gospel. From almost their first words of testimony, she wept with relief and belief, as if hearing a long-awaited signal of hope. They left her home that first evening calling her "Sister Miller." She even wept at that.

In the second discussion, they told Sister Miller about the

restoration of priesthood to the earth. She accepted this without question and then surprised the elders by asking, "Does the priesthood have power to do miracles, like when Jesus healed the sick?"

The elders assured her that the priesthood was just as powerful now as it ever was.

"And you hold this priesthood?" she asked with some tension in her voice. They nodded at this but wondered if they had gotten themselves into a situation that required more than just words of faith. They soon learned that they had. "Well, then," she said with the tears beginning again, "would you heal me?"

Sister Miller had taken the step of faith Mormon speaks of: If God was willing to bless with power in centuries past, nothing has changed—unless it is faith. He has not changed, for he was perfect then and still is. Such faith is a compliment to God. It credits him with fairness, maturity, and power. In a way, she was teaching the missionaries.

A serious physical condition threatened Sister Miller's life. They were moved as she pled to be healed so that she might raise her daughters and now raise them in the true Church. After a day of fasting the elders returned, full of faith. They bestowed a priesthood blessing. The Lord chose to heal Sister Miller almost immediately.

Then came another lesson. Sister Miller's conclusion from all this was very simple: "If the Lord can heal my body, he can help me in every part of life. He will help me spiritually and financially. He will bless my little girls. If we will just be good and have faith, we won't have to worry. That one miracle proves I will always be treated well."

86.
THE ONE WAY OF FREEDOM

Behold, this is a choice land, and whatsoever nation shall possess it shall be free from bondage, and from captivity, and from all other nations under heaven, if they will but serve the God of the land, who is Jesus Christ. (Ether 2:12.)

At just the right time in Nephite history, King Mosiah suggested a new political system—a democratic republic. And to make sure that some future group could not get the people to vote away their own freedoms, he proposed a core of law that could not be changed—a constitution. This deep part would give the nation its character. Without it, liberty could be overturned by the slightest breeze of confusion.

But what should be the essence of this unchangeable constitution? It should be rooted in the wisdom of God's commandments.[1] Not only would there be a foundation, but the foundation would be wise— reinforced with steel.

A new nation has a perfect right to set the commandments of God at the heart of their laws. He is, after all, the greatest governor in the universe. To ignore that wisdom in nation-building is an arrogant form of suicide.[2]

Lehi's family were promised they would have every necessary blessing. They would be wrapped in the protection of heaven. Their part of the

bargain was stated too simply to misunderstand, too often to forget: Keep the commandments.[3]

Freedom isn't free, of course.[4] And what is more, it isn't
man-made. The Lord arranges things so that only he can make a
person or a people free—so that "none could deliver them but
the Lord their God."[5]

But, in spite of their constitution, the Nephites threw away
almost everything within some sixty years. Looking back, they
could see the stages of their undoing:

They came to view God's commandments as nonsense.[6]

They replaced the inspired constitution with "corrupted"
laws.[7]

Living those corrupt laws made them "a wicked people."[8]

Blending with this society, church members dwindled in
faith.[9]

"The Spirit of the Lord did no more preserve them."[10]

Of course, none of this had to happen. Back in Mosiah's day,
for example, the Spirit of the Lord preserved the nation constantly. Mosiah's people would certainly have been brought into
bondage "were it not for the interposition of their all-wise
Creator."[11] "Interposition" is a big word but a good one—God
"positioned" himself between his people and the threat that faced
them.

"Behold, he did deliver them because they did humble themselves before him; and because they cried mightily unto him he
did deliver them out of bondage; and thus doth the Lord work
with his power in all cases among the children of men, extending
the arm of mercy towards them that put their trust in him."[12]

There is no need for any nation to be in bondage. All are
invited to live as these Nephites lived. That is how the Lord
works "in all cases."

87.
BELIEVE AND SEE

Come unto me, . . . and I will show unto you the greater things, the knowledge which is hid up because of unbelief. (Ether 4:13.)

It was one of those unpleasant discussions. The family was not arguing, but every point of view was different, and none seemed to be the answer. This was a large family, and they had to move soon. They had looked at both houses available in their price range, and neither seemed to fit their basic needs. As the parents and older children each tried to explain how a particular house might be adapted, they found themselves stopping mid-sentence, lacking conviction. In one of those moments of confusion, five-year-old Erica said quietly, "Why don't you just ask the Lord? He knows what to do."

Everybody already knew that, of course. Mom and Dad had already prayed about this matter more than once. But Erica's tone suggested they were missing something. It was not Erica's idea but Erica's faith that changed everything.

Now it wasn't, "Well, Heavenly Father, here we are again, praying about the same problem, the hopeless one that we keep bringing up." Instead, it was, "Father, we are sure that the right answer is visible to thee. We are ready to do our part to see it."

Another house soon came to their

attention, one they would not have discovered except by a blessing from heaven. The members of that family believe that this blessing came because of mightier faith, inspired by a little girl.

To believe is to make a perfectly trusting assumption about God: "I don't know what he's talking about, but I know that he knows what he's talking about."

For all people, light sometimes shines on certain truths. When this happens, they can ignore it or look into it. The choice to ignore can become a bad habit. Moroni called it a "veil of unbelief," because when we do not believe we cannot see. Unbelief draws a heavy curtain across our view, which, he said "doth cause you to remain in your awful state of . . . blindness of mind."[1]

We can't see until we look. We won't even look unless we think we might see something. A pessimistic outlook is no "outlook" at all. The unbelieving view is self-imposed blindness. It is no "view" at all.

For example, the question of who we really are is answered by the most wondrous truth in the universe. But the saddest fact in the world is that most of mankind do not know who they are. Even those who have some idea about it may not really believe it—they don't feel that they are actually children of God. What keeps mankind from having this knowledge? "It hath not come unto you, because of unbelief."[2] Unbelief ruins everything.[3]

Unbelief is a blindfold for people who are already poor of sight. Faith is a corrective lens, a microscope, a telescope.[4] Unbelief is darkness. Our faith persuades heaven to turn on the lights.

88.
A MIGHTY ANCHOR

Whoso believeth in God might with surety hope for a better world, yea, even a place at the right hand of God, which hope cometh of faith, maketh an anchor to the souls of men, which would make them sure and steadfast, always abounding in good works, being led to glorify God. (Ether 12:4.)

There are different kinds of hope. If your car runs out of fuel, you could "hope" your car will float the next twenty miles to a gas station. If that works, you hope not to upset the police, the aviation authorities, or other drivers. You hope to make a nice landing. If you are going to do all that, you might as well just stay where you are and hope the gas station floats those twenty miles to you.

The kind of hope Moroni speaks of is "surety." If you have the faith to be steadfast, you know where you stand with God. "Abounding in good works" prepares you for "a better world." You can count on it. You are not waiting for a car to fly. You are walking to the gas station, and you know what that means. You will get there, that's what it means. You don't give up and sit down and have a nervous collapse somewhere along the way. You keep walking, and as you get closer to your destination, your hope is more assured. "I'm getting closer. This is getting exciting. Passing drivers may call out insults. Dogs may threaten. Darkness may fall. Candy shops may allure. Shoes may come untied. But I will not be diverted. I know what walking does: It gets you there."

Edie is called "the anchor" by her swimming team. That seems a little strange for a water sport. But Edie doesn't sink to the bottom. She is the one they count on. Her opponents think she's a little scary. When they see Edie swim, their hope gets watery. When it's Edie's turn to go in the relay, she has a way of catching up and coming in first. She is "the anchor" because she gives hope.

Of course, our real "anchor man" is Christ. He is the hope of those who are on his team, who jump in and do their best.[1] He is infinitely dependable and firm. When he waits, it is firmly. When the time comes to act, he acts firmly. His resolve is firm, his results are firm.

To the adversary, hope in Christ is scary, unsettling. For example, when Ammon stood up to a gang of sheep rustlers, his hope was in no way wishy or shy. It was decisive, strident, and fearless.[2] That was unsettling to his foes. A firm hope is the best way to face opposition and partner with heaven.

On the surface, the storm tugs and slashes. The ship strains and trembles from side to side. In the depths, all that violence is chained to one spot, one grip on the ocean floor. The sum of stress and turmoil that beats against a life can be transferred to one solid anchor—the Savior we have decided to trust with all our hearts. Our Anchor may not still the wind, but he will hold us still in the wind.

89.
THE POWER TO CHANGE

I give unto men weakness that they may be humble; and my grace is sufficient for all men that humble themselves before me; for if they humble themselves before me, and have faith in me, then will I make weak things become strong unto them. (Ether 12:27.)

Nothing in all of nature is so magnificent as the human capacity for change. Our Father arranged a great atonement to foster our progress from weak to strong, but he also made us capable of moving across that spectrum. The way to harness the power of change is to humble ourselves. Fortunately, the very weaknesses that signal our need for change can inspire the humility we need to qualify for it.

"And if men come unto me I will show unto them their weakness."[1]

In the world of strength competition, there is an event called "the farmer's walk." It requires the contestant to carry a very heavy object in each hand and simply walk as far as he can without a rest. After a block or so, very strong people—people who can normally lift cars and throw boulders over walls—are trembling and stumbling and wilting as if they had no strength at all. They don't look or feel very strong.

And of course there is the real farmer's walk that has been going on for thousands of years. Good and noble people extract their survival from the harsh elements. Sometimes they barely get by, or even starve.

Meanwhile the well-fed may look down on them, thinking them to be weak, unsteady, unsuccessful. Weak? No, anyone would struggle under such a burden.

"Fools mock, but they shall mourn; and my grace is sufficient for the meek."[2]

Fools find another person's weakness an excuse for comparisons, for ego-propping and amusement. But those fools will someday look again and see what was really going on—strongmen and strongwomen were loaded down with handicaps. They were like a majestic racehorse hampered by extra riders.

To train for strength, what do you do? You face enough resistance to challenge you, to make you feel weak, to exhaust you, to require recovery and rebuilding.

Our God is a strength trainer, the most experienced and successful coach in the universe. This Trainer of ours is master of worlds and systems beyond measuring. He is not intimidated at the thought of helping us grow to galactic size. Nephi reasoned, "Ye know that by his word he can cause the rough places to be made smooth, and smooth places shall be broken up. O, then, why is it, that ye can be so hard in your hearts?"[3] The power for change is there if we will humble ourselves.

The weaknesses he bestows on us are but weights designed to enlarge our powers. As any strength trainer could tell us, the growth cycle is slow for muscles and even slower for tendons. If the spirit is only as complex and potent as the body, this could take weeks or years. If the spirit is far greater than the body—and it is—it could take a lifetime.

90.
THE POWER TO REJOICE

The Lord said unto me: If they have not charity it mattereth not unto thee, thou hast been faithful; wherefore, thy garments shall be made clean. And because thou hast seen thy weakness thou shalt be made strong, even unto the sitting down in the place which I have prepared in the mansions of my Father. (Ether 12:37.)

Moroni knew that latter-day people would be learned and demanding.[1] Here he was, drafting a book of scripture from various sources on non-erasable metal, and doing so while living in almost desperate circumstances. He could only guess that his readers would be critical of the outcome.

But there comes a point in our work where we have done enough. At that point, we would be out of line to stew about it any further. The Lord will expect others to be charitable when reviewing our best effort. And anyway, the book would not change one life more if Moroni had been free to make another draft.

Though the book would be published to a generation of critics, and though it might have some imperfection, Moroni was told, "It mattereth not unto thee, thou hast been faithful." He is invited to be satisfied with what he has done, to rejoice that he did his part well. It is the Lord's book, not Moroni's. At some point, the Lord must worry about details.

In an incident from Nephi's life, we see the choice for rejoicing when he easily could have pouted and chosen to be depressed. The circulation to his hands and feet had been cut off by tight bands for days. He had been tied down by his own brothers on the deck of a ship that he had built for their benefit. This man who never complains could only say, "Great was the soreness thereof." This was a chance for bitterness if there ever was one, for this was real abuse.

But he chose another path: "I did look unto my God, and I did praise him all the day long; and I did not murmur against the Lord because of mine afflictions." That response entitled him to the Spirit of the Lord and the power of the priesthood. He was able to take the helm of that ship and to call down the power of God. Only then could "a great calm" halt the storm that nearly killed a whole nation before it could be born.[2]

What if Nephi had not chosen to rejoice? History would now read differently in the Book of Mormon, or perhaps there would be no Book of Mormon to read.

To react darkly to the unfriendly and unfair world is to start writing a dark history of our lives and families. We shape the story we leave behind. We shape the long history of generations to come. When the opportunity to be bitter comes along—and it comes along often for most of us—it is also an opportunity to be better, and to set in motion a better story. And we even choose one of the heroes for that story.

When we are willing to rejoice, the power to rejoice will come to us. And then a "great calm" settles over our own journey to promised land.[3]

91.
POWER AS WELL AS PRIESTHOOD

Ye shall call on the Father in my name, in mighty prayer; and after ye have done this ye shall have power that to him upon whom ye shall lay your hands, ye shall give the Holy Ghost; and in my name shall ye give it, for thus do mine apostles.

(Moroni 2:2.)

The promise here is not about whether priesthood holders can perform ordinances. Moroni is quoting the words Jesus spoke to seasoned leaders. With them, and the other members of the Church, that is a settled matter. Of course the ordinance is valid.

But what kind of experience is attending that ordinance? Should it not be a powerful experience, an unforgettable one? Yes, the ordinance was accepted in heaven. But while we are performing a sacred act, should we not make it a holy one as well, one that will edify everyone present? It is possible to do both. When using Christ's holy priesthood, we can have his holy power with us as well.

"Thus do mine apostles," he says. If we've been around an apostle, we know that this is their pattern. They fine-tune their worthiness. They call upon the Father in private. They make sure the Spirit is with them. The ordinances are not only authorized and legal in the eyes of God. They are also inspiring, attended by a sweet power. All priesthood holders are invited to go about their own priesthood work according to this apostolic pattern.

Organizations are in the habit of appointing representatives. There are "congressional reps" and "company reps" and "division reps" and "district reps" and "sales reps" and "agency reps" and even "drug reps" who introduce new medicines to the doctors. But seldom does a "rep" have the power of the whole organization. If a representative of the electrical power company comes to your home, you can't plug a radio into his shoulder. (You can, but the sound you hear wouldn't be from the radio.)

By contrast, the Lord desires to fill his servants with power that can reach others. His servants are then not only legal representatives but also carriers of his influence, vessels of his power—"instruments."[1] To each son of Mosiah and each of their mission companions, the Lord said, "I will make an instrument of thee in my hands unto the salvation of many souls."[2]

No instance of this principle is more important than in giving a blessing. For example, a simple father's blessing can affect the story of a child's life and the long history that rises out of that story. After Lehi had given a blessing to one of his sons, he said, "Because of my blessing the Lord God will not suffer that ye shall perish; wherefore, he will be merciful unto you and unto your seed forever."[3]

"Forever" is quite a result to come from a blessing that took perhaps three or four minutes to bestow. But of course, this could not have happened if Lehi were only a legal representative and nothing more. He had prepared himself. As he laid his hands on the head of his son, Lehi was an instrument in the hands of God.

92.
DISCERNMENT EQUAL TO THE BATTLE

All things which are good cometh of God; and that which is evil cometh of the devil; for the devil is an enemy unto God, and fighteth against him continually, and inviteth and enticeth to sin, and to do that which is evil continually. (Moroni 7:12.)

Satan and his hosts are busy these days. There is a vicious assault taking place. A terrible war is brewing. It has already cut down millions of victims. It will grow hotter. If we don't want to be another casualty in this war, we have to learn to detect evil.

The way to detect evil is certainly not to partake of it. That would be like checking for rat poison with a taste test.

The promise is that evil can always be discerned. We may see it from a distance. We may smell it from a distance. We may know it simply by its source. This is a wonderful feature of discernment. We can detect the danger from a distance.

There is a science called "toxicology"—the study of water, food, and other substances to learn whether they are harmful. This field of study began in the fifteenth century with a man named Paracelsus, a scientist of the day. It has now become an amazing discipline that can find the tiniest trace of toxin almost anywhere.

But before Paracelsus came along, people could stay out of trouble in most cases by using their noses. "This stream has a funny smell to it," a mother would say, "so we aren't going to drink from it, no matter how thirsty we get!"

Or, "This meat smells bad," a child might say. "Then don't put it in your mouth!" the father would quickly answer.

"A bitter fountain cannot bring forth good water; neither can a good fountain bring forth bitter water."[1]

As the eyes and nose allow us to keep a distance from toxins, we have a spiritual sense that—if honored—will detect evil before it gets into our systems.

But if this spiritual sense is dishonored, it is disabled. An extreme case is when people around the Son of God ignored the signals that he was good and holy. "The world, because of their iniquity, shall judge him to be a thing of naught; wherefore they scourge him, and he suffereth it; and they smite him, and he suffereth it. Yea, they spit upon him, and he suffereth it."[2] How could they have been so absolutely and terribly wrong? Nephi gave the answer: "Because of their iniquity." Broken noses, we might say.

The price of lost discernment can be infinite. Jacob warned about the "awfulness of yielding to the enticings of that cunning one." Awful because the damage can be so crippling to a human soul. Awful because happiness is replaced by a more or less constant misery. Awful because the misery can last so long.

Our defense is the spiritual toxicology that Jacob calls being "spiritually-minded." "Remember," he declared, "to be carnally-minded is death, and to be spiritually-minded is life eternal."[3] We win the war by honoring our wonderful ability to see and smell danger from a distance.

93.
GOODNESS LEADS TO MORE GOODNESS

Whatsoever thing persuadeth men to do evil, and believe not in Christ, and deny him, and serve not God, . . . ye may know with a perfect knowledge it is of the devil; for after this manner doth the devil work, for he persuadeth no man to do good, no, not one; neither do his angels; neither do they who subject themselves unto him. (Moroni 7:17.)

In this caution we find a promise: Evil sources are always evil. The devil never sponsors good.[1] So, if you are invited to do good, trust the invitation. That is one way to discern the Spirit of Christ. If I am prompted to do good—to build up my Father's work or to bless my fellow beings—that's the right spirit.[2] Good invitations lead only to more good invitations.

In the days before flashlights, Clark and his brother used to beg Mother to let them explore the caves near their home. Father had passed away, and Mother didn't feel fit enough to go in with them. "But," she reasoned, "it's sure they'll go in there sometime. Maybe it should be with my permission." When she decided that, she thought of a plan.

"Okay, boys," she explained as they stood on a rock above the dark entrance, "we've heard stories about people gettin' lost down there, and I'll not have you bein' one of 'em. So you're not just goin' in with torches. I'll be out here with the rope tied to this rock, feedin' rope out to you. You're both goin' to be attached to the other end the whole time."

"But what if the rope isn't long enough and we want to go in farther?" Clark asked.

His mother's voice sizzled as she spoke. "If you get loose of this rope in there, and I ever see you again . . ." Six long ropes, tied end to end, would take them far enough.

Clark remembers, "No one thought about how smoky it would get with those torches burning. We finally got in a place where we couldn't see for all the smoke, and we could hardly breathe. That's where we decided to put out the torches altogether."

"Now the interesting thing is," Clark continued, "there were pieces of old broken twine and string lying all around in those passages. But we could tell Mother's rope from all that other flimsy stuff. It made us feel pretty secure as we followed it out."

The influence of Christ is stronger than all the others. And it is the only one that leads out of this dark place, back to our waiting Father.

"Whatsoever thing persuadeth men to do good is of me; for good cometh of none save it be of me. I am the same that leadeth men to all good."[3]

That is the great secret about goodness. All of it can be traced back to him. If we follow it and nothing else, it will lead to him and no one else.

Sometimes he plants goodness in us and lets it expand by our effort. Or, he may plant it in others and let us find it in them. Either way, it leads us to the Light of the World. Without him and his wise, pulsing goodness, there would be no good in this world. Our job is to keep following it.

94.
CHARITY LASTS

Cleave unto charity, which is the greatest of all, for all things must fail—but charity is the pure love of Christ, and it endureth forever; and whoso is found possessed of it at the last day, it shall be well with him. (Moroni 7:46–47.)

Are people more patient and loving at home than anywhere else? That sounds reasonable enough. But we haven't seen it very often. It is rare.

Our family members aren't harder to love than other folks. They aren't worse; they are probably better. But we know them. Facts can be confusing. Too much information to process here. These people are imperfect, and we know it. We know the details.

How often has a teacher had an experience like this? "I surely enjoy having your daughter in my class."

After a confused pause, the mother asks, "My daughter? You mean Melissa?"

"Sure, she's great," the teacher answers sincerely. "Respectful, thoughtful, strong testimony." The mother nods politely and walks away, wondering if the teacher is all there.

Knowing the mortal details about a human soul can distract us from the eternal details. We may focus on the mighty struggles and fail to admire the mighty strength.

Another reason why love at home is hard: The people there accept us

190

even if we aren't perfectly affectionate with them. So we may not work at love in the home the way we work at it in the public eye. Why try hard if they will still love us even if we don't try hard?

How often does this happen? Mom has had a long and hard and hurried day—a very normal day. It is best not to make a lot of noise. It is best not to ask what's for dinner. It is best to bear no bad tidings. In fact, no tidings at all would be wise. Give her some space. Clean something up somewhere. And then the phone rings.

"Oh, hello. . . . I'm doing great, how are you? . . . Sure, I've got time to talk . . ." And so on. Who is calling? It could be anyone. Her sister, a neighbor, a total stranger, most anyone.

We have mentioned two reasons why our homes are not always showcases of charity. So if we are to be like Christ, who loves perfectly, what can we do about these reasons?

1. If we know our "loved ones" when they are not at their best, we can do as Christ does. He views them as eternal beings struggling with awkward mortal problems. With that view, he loves them forever.

2. If we are not always at our best either, we can do as Christ does. Love is his life. He doesn't wait for it to "happen." He doesn't take a break from it. He is at his best. Always.

If charity were easy, it would be everywhere. But it is "the greatest of all," the greatest attainment, perhaps the last attainment. Pure love is an excellence of heavenly beings, which is why their joy is greater than ours. If the home lasts forever, and if charity lasts forever, then here is a match made in heaven.

95.
A Universal Gift

Pray unto the Father with all the energy of heart, that ye may be filled with this love, which he hath bestowed upon all who are true followers of his Son, Jesus Christ; that ye may become the sons of God; that when he shall appear we shall be like him, . . . that we may be purified even as he is pure. (Moroni 7:48.)

We might have known: mighty prayer—praying "with all the energy of heart"—is needed in order that something so important might fill us. But that is also very good news. No matter how ill-qualified we seem to be, no matter how unlikely that this could ever be a part of our personality, charity can be "bestowed upon" us. That is worth praying about.

We don't have to drop everything else we have been working on and praying for in order to be filled with charity. All the traits of godliness grow and blend alongside each other, like parts written for various instruments in a symphony. For example, knowledge doesn't sound very good when blurted out alone, without the supporting notes of charity and faith. Honesty needs the balancing presence of self-control and kindness.

When we pray for an uncle or a child or a struggling neighbor or a woman in our ward who has an illness, those prayers are acts of love. We pray for a forgiveness of our sins. But we realize that this calls for a spirit of tolerance in our own hearts toward others, and so we make a plea for that spirit. Somehow, our prayers to the Father are never far away from love. He can hardly answer any of our important prayers without filling us with love.

Some members of Lehi's family were not easy to live with, and wading through afflictions didn't necessarily make it easier. But the righteous members of that family managed to love their thorny relatives. Where did that love come from? No doubt, they prayed for it, in specific ways and indirect ways. They lived for that gift by their daily efforts to keep the commandments. So it distilled on them. We find them kind and patient—amazingly patient—when Laman and certain others got violent and out of control. It was a miracle.

That love settles on people as they live and give and pray day by day. The twenty-year-old girl who leaves bad habits behind and transforms her life just happens to start loving her family with a tenderness neither she nor they have known in her before. Christ is involved in this. She is being "purified even as he is pure."[1] It is a miracle.

Keith, a reformed alcoholic, and Terrance, a formerly bitter critic of the Church, are now both active in the Church. They are on a priesthood assignment, weeding flowerbeds around the ward meetinghouse. During those three hours, they end up sharing their conversion stories, expressing concern over sorrows they each have for wayward children, each man feeling a soaring love for the other, determining that his new friend will have an interest in his prayers. Thus, in the ancient gospel pattern, their love makes them the "the sons of God."[2] It is a miracle.

The miracle is bestowed on all the "true followers" of Christ. And it makes them even truer.

96.
LAUNCHING A WONDERFUL AND LAWFUL JOURNEY

The remission of sins bringeth meekness, and lowliness of heart; and because of meekness and lowliness of heart cometh the visitation of the Holy Ghost, which Comforter filleth with hope and perfect love, which love endureth by diligence unto prayer, until the end shall come, when all the saints shall dwell with God. (Moroni 8:26.)

At the close of one of the most enlightening lives ever lived, Mormon spoke of a lawful and wonderful path—a path of spiritual growth. He had seen it in himself and others. He noticed it all through the old records of generations past. It was consistent in wartime and peace, poverty and plenty, with young and old, Nephite and Lamanite.

We are fortunate to have Mormon's little summary of the path—in a way, distilling everything he had written. It begins with the remission of sins. It leads at last to the presence of God—to associate closely with him forever.

There is always more than one way to divide up a journey. But whether it is in four parts or three or thirteen, the movement must be in a certain direction and go through lawful points along the way.

Mormon's summary goes something like this: (1) Cleansed of sin, (2) Meekness, (3) The Comforter, (4) Hope and Love, (5) Prayer, (6) Diligence to the end, (7) Dwell with God.[1]

If we trace the journey backward from the presence of God, we see that a person simply will not "dwell with God" unless he or she "endureth by diligence." And Mormon has learned that a life of enduring righteousness is not possible without enduring prayer.

Experience shows that without the fuel of hope and love, we just won't continue in prayer. Can you just manufacture that sweet, comforting fuel on your own? Not at all.

The hope must come from the "visitation of the Holy Ghost," the Comforter who gives us reasons to press on. The journey absolutely demands that the Holy Ghost join us early in the trek.

If the companionship of the Holy Ghost is rich enough to carry us through our journey into the presence of God—and it most surely is!—then the burning question is this: How does a weak mortal go about receiving that companion? The answer is right there in Mormon's words. The Holy Ghost is attracted to "meekness and lowliness of heart." The years of life, the lessons of a thousand other lives, and the whisperings of inspiration all declare this truth: meekness invites the Comforter.

But this is not the meekness of shame or embarrassment. It is not the humiliation that precedes repentance but the humility that comes after repentance. It is not the remorse that begs for a remission of sins but the stunned relief that melts us to our knees when sins are remitted. It is gratitude and worship. This meekness that attracts our holy companion is strong rather than weak, joyous rather than regretful, ready to move forward rather than frozen to our past in shame or fear.

So, the first step in the wonderful, lawful journey to God is to become clean.

97.
PERFECT REST FOR THE MIND

Be faithful in Christ; and may not the things which I have written grieve thee, to weigh thee down unto death; but may Christ lift thee up, and may his sufferings and death, and the showing his body unto our fathers, and his mercy and long-suffering, and the hope of his glory and of eternal life, rest in your mind forever. (Moroni 9:25.)

We cannot quite imagine the specter of inhumanity and horror that accompanied the Nephite nation to its last gasping moments. And though Mormon describes it, we can hardly stand to read it. These people imposing ghastly tortures upon the innocent, these sponsors of wanton brutality and senseless cannibalism, were members of the human family to which we belong. They were former friends of our friend Mormon.

When the unthinkable happens before the sensitive eyes of Mormon and Moroni and their brothers and sisters in the faith, where could they look for sanity? When almost all that was spread before them was not merely natural calamity but also unnatural ferocity, what comfort could they find for their minds?

And not only them. We live in times that share some of the same dark tones as theirs. When we begin to realize the degree of sorrow, agony, and horror that stalks our world—and we can only begin to grasp it no matter how many news articles we see—what could bring us comfort, except to know that it is only temporary?

Though it was there in centuries past and still prevails now and may continue tomorrow, it helps to know that for each individual sufferer it lasts only for a time, never to be repeated again. That individual's life will persist on and on forever in comfort and luxury, in conditions far higher and finer than our present world. They will each rejoice in the gifts and relief and lifting power of Christ.

The message from Mormon to Moroni and you and me is: Let that hope of something infinitely better burn brightly while the cycle of sorrow lasts on a while. Remember that this will not last long.

If some sorrowful fact is to hold our attention, let it be the suffering and death of Christ. Let us be oriented to that one instance of trembling, and let us never forget that it ended in triumph. Let us recall that his suffering will be the means of vanquishing all other suffering—all of it.

This philosophy—to be mindful of Christ's offering while we walk through the unhappy world—is what we adopt in partaking of the sacrament. We "always remember"[1] the realities that a little bread and water bring to the mind of a disciple.

"May the grace of God the Father, whose throne is high in the heavens, and our Lord Jesus Christ, who sitteth on the right hand of his power, until all things shall become subject unto him, be, and abide with you forever. Amen."[2]

As far as we know, these words were the last that Mormon wrote to his son. And they were his fatherly benediction on us as well. Until Christ calms all other sorrows, let him calm yours.

98.
THE POWER OF CONFIRMATION

By the power of the Holy Ghost ye may know the truth of all things. (Moroni 10:5.)

After all those eons of premortal preparation, we must have had big reasons for wanting a physical body. Look at all the trouble God has taken to provide it for us, and all the trouble we are taking to add this new side to our nature.

The body can never compare to the spirit, the real us, the part that makes us who we are. And yet, we didn't want to go forever without a body.

A little family came into the house after a long trip. "The house is cold," said one of the children. "I'm hungry," said another.

"Be ye warmed and filled," Daddy called out from the basement.

"What's that supposed to mean?" the oldest child asked.

Mother smiled. "It means that Daddy is getting a fire going in the furnace, and I'm going to start making some bread. In an hour or two, we won't be cold or hungry. Till then, maybe Daddy wants you to plan on it. You feel better already, don't you?"

It probably did help some. They could count on the word of their parents. In their minds, they had a confirmation of a truth their bodies would have to wait to enjoy. But the confirmation alone would help them wait.

As Sariah and her husband Lehi waited for the return of their sons from Jerusalem, they had assurances that all would be well. Sariah heard her husband bear testimony: "I know that the Lord will deliver my sons out of the hands of Laban, and bring them down again unto us in the wilderness." Did this comfort Sariah? Of course it did: "And after this manner of language did my father, Lehi, comfort my mother, Sariah."

Her husband's testimony, and the power of the Holy Ghost that attended it, wasn't the same as having her sons back. But it confirmed the truth to her mind. Her arms and eyes would have to wait to enjoy that truth, and then the comfort would expand. Upon the return of their sons, Sariah and her husband were able to bask in a knowledge that was confirmed both physically and spiritually. "Their joy was full. . . . They did rejoice exceedingly."[1]

So a woman of faith was comforted even before she had a perfect knowledge. If faith is willing to precede the miracle, then comfort can precede the miracle too. Where there is faith, there will be comfort in a confirmation from the Holy Ghost alone.

The power of the Holy Ghost can certify many important truths. Just one of these is the certainty that the Book of Mormon is the word of God. Everyone is entitled to know that.[2] When this confirmation comes, we can stake our lives on it.

And then we can turn to the same source for a confirmation of other truths—truths that our physical senses may have to wait to enjoy.[3]

99.

NEVER A QUESTION OF POWER

Remember that he is the same yesterday, today, and forever, and that all these gifts of which I have spoken, which are spiritual, never will be done away, even as long as the world shall stand, only according to the unbelief of the children of men. (Moroni 10:19.)

Many parents sit down now and then to decide what gifts they can afford for their children. They have a birthday budget for the year based on how much money they have and how many of their children are having birthdays this year.[1] Maybe the budget varies as they have more money or more children.

But that isn't how it is with our Father's gift budget. Yes, he has a lot of children, but on the other hand he can afford anything. He doesn't have to measure out the gifts cautiously out of fear of going broke.

If he had a trillion children and only a trillion dollars' worth of gifts, this would be a problem. The budget would limit each of us to a dollar's worth. But he has an infinitude to give—his resources are simply unlimited. That means that each one of his trillion children—or a trillion trillion children—might be granted an infinitude of gifts.

Even the gifts themselves are numberless, no doubt. The list we find in Moroni 10:9–18 is surely just a sample.[2]

Several verses after the promise

we have quoted, Moroni gives us this striking quotation from Christ himself: "If ye have faith ye can do all things which are expedient unto me."[3]

It is never a question of whether he is powerful enough or generous enough to grant one of his gifts. The question is only whether that gift is "expedient" in his view. Something is expedient if it moves things along toward some end, a way of accomplishing some goal. When we seek a gift from his hand, the goal has to be acceptable to him, and the means for reaching it has to be wise and right in his sight.

Sometimes the gift we seek is wrong because the goal is self-ambitious or silly. He may not be very impressed if we want help in becoming a soap opera star or in buying our very own castle. If we ask for the gift of tongues so that we can play bingo throughout Europe, the gift will be withheld.

And if the goal is right, what if the gift we seek is not a wise means for reaching it? We may want to help the poor, and ask for the gift of prophecy so we can make millions of dollars in the stock market. Maybe this will not fit our Father's plan.

But though some gifts or goals are not expedient, countless others are. We may sometime seek the gift to be healed of physical illness, emotional trouble, or spiritual weakness, and find that we have chosen the right time for the right gift.[4] Many times we are given the inspiration to sense what gift would be expedient for us in the Lord's eyes.[5] Then is the time to exercise mighty faith.

100.

BECOMING SPOTLESS AND PERFECT

Come unto Christ, and be perfected in him, and deny yourselves of all ungodliness; and if ye shall deny yourselves of all ungodliness, and love God with all your might, mind and strength, then is his grace sufficient for you, that by his grace ye may be perfect in Christ; and if by the grace of God ye are perfect in Christ, ye can in nowise deny the power of God. (Moroni 10:32.)

We have come to just about the last promise declared in a majestic bookful of promises. This one is stated as clearly as we could desire. It offers a blessing as great as anything we could ask. And there are but two requirements, both of them as reachable as anyone could want.

The blessing is perfection. At the close of the great book, its words leave no question about the gospel aim. It is perfection of the most desirable kind—becoming "perfect in Christ." Perfected in his capable and artistic hands, perfected to the uncompromising standard of his justice, perfected in principle and light, in patience and power.[1]

In the meantime, it is hard enough to just drive across town without breaking some law or other. Anything even approaching perfection is beyond our native powers. But we are not in the gospel covenant on our own powers.

"Then are ye sanctified in Christ by the grace of God, through the shedding of the blood of Christ, which is in the covenant of the Father."[2]

The very word "covenant" reminds us we are not on our own. Our partner is a God.

If his part in the partnership is to perfect us, what is left for us to do? Two simple tasks: "Deny yourselves of all ungodliness," and "Love God with all your might, mind, and strength." No matter how weak we are, we can do those two things. No matter how far behind we seem to be in the human trek toward perfection, we can handle that much.

Suppose a king told us he would give us a gleaming castle if only we would clean up around our little hut. We cannot build a castle. We may not even have a can of paint. But we can pick up the litter. That will take some effort, but for a castle . . .

The Lord asks that we deny ourselves of litter—the ungodly actions and influences that are under our control. If we have trouble with ungodly language, we don't have to study grammar or become famous orators. We are only asked to keep the coarse verbal litter from coming out of our mouths. When we get that under control, we can go to work on ungodly thoughts. So it is with all the unworthy elements that make us imperfect. Remove what we can. That doesn't make us perfect, but it frees Christ to perfect us.

If, that is, we will do that one other thing—love him as much as we can. We are not asked to love him as much as someone else can, but with whatever might, mind, and strength we possess. It may not be a lot just yet, but he asks that we love him with whatever there is. In turn, he will not be restrained in expressing his love for us. He will, with all his might, mind, and strength, make sure that we grow perfect.

101.
CONCLUSION: AN APPOINTMENT WITH PROPHETS

And now I bid unto all, farewell. I soon go to rest in the paradise of God, until my spirit and body shall again reunite, and I am brought forth triumphant through the air, to meet you before the pleasing bar of the great Jehovah, the Eternal Judge of both quick and dead. Amen. (Moroni 10:34.)

In a day just as real as any day we have ever known, we will meet with Moroni and other prophets. We will look them in the eye, no doubt. We will report on what we have done about the book they wrote. And we will be in the presence of One even greater than the prophets.[1] If we have been faithful, it will be a wonderful day.

The quarterback judges where the receiver will be and throws the ball to that spot. The receiver judges where the ball will come down and runs to that spot. The tackler tries to get to that spot too.

Astronomers use more math than football players do, but it's the same idea. They draw some fancy lines and predict when the earth is going to be near Mars.

Aerospace scientists calculate where the moon will be and point the landing craft in that direction. They figure out where the earth is going to be a few days later and point the returning shuttle to that exact place.

This judging where things are going to be is an important business, but never so important as when we try to understand how the great plan is going to wind up, and where we are going to be when the closing scenes occur.

Two friends plan to meet each other somewhere downtown. On the cell phone, one asks where the other is right now. "Let's see, you're heading south on Main right now, and the traffic is slow? Well then, I'll head east on Third Avenue, and we should both be at the library in about ten minutes. Let's meet there." In their minds, they draw a little map with lines that should meet.

We follow Moroni's advice and "remember how merciful the Lord hath been unto the children of men, . . . and ponder it in [our] hearts."[2] We see that he has been true to every promise he ever made. If he kept those promises, he will keep all the others. They all require the same power and goodness. And he changes not.[3]

We can tell how this is going to end up, can't we? "The eternal purposes of the Lord shall roll on, until all his promises shall be fulfilled."[4] If we are following the divine plan, we can draw a line in our minds and see that we are going to be in the right place with our friends the prophets and our Friend the Christ when all the promises are fulfilled.

"You and I shall stand face to face before his bar," Nephi said, "and ye shall know that I have been commanded of him to write these things. . . . Farewell until that great day shall come."[5]

NOTES

INTRODUCTION:
A BOOK OF HOPE

1. 2 Nephi 9:53.

1. THE POWER OF DELIVERANCE

1. Mosiah 21.
2. Mosiah 21:13.
3. Mosiah 29:20.
4. Alma 36:3.
5. Alma 38:5.

2. HE PREPARES A WAY

1. 1 Nephi 3:31–4:3.
2. 1 Nephi 3:7.
3. 1 Nephi 2:19–20; 2 Nephi 4:33; Ether 2:25.
4. 1 Nephi 21:5.
5. Alma 13:5.
6. Alma 7:9.

3. THE PROPHET OF PROPHETS

1. 1 Nephi 22:20–21.
2. 1 Nephi 20:17. See also Jacob 4:10.
3. 2 Nephi 25:18–20.
4. 2 Nephi 21:2.

4. THE TIMELESS RIGHT TO KNOW

1. 1 Nephi 11:1.
2. 2 Nephi 9:50. See also Alma 5:46; Ether 4:11.

5. A HOLY BIRTH

1. 1 Nephi 15:36.
2. Alma 32:37–42; 3 Nephi 14:17–20.

3. 1 Nephi 11:16, 21–22.
4. 1 Nephi 11:7.
5. Mosiah 3:5.

6. A HOLY LIFE

1. Mosiah 3:5; 7:27.
2. Mosiah 14:2–3.
3. 3 Nephi 27:13.
4. 3 Nephi 11:11.

7. JUDGED BY THOSE WHO KNOW

1. Mormon 3:18–20.
2. Moroni 10:33.
3. 2 Nephi 2:6.
4. Alma 13:9; 41:14.

8. HE WILL MANIFEST HIMSELF

1. 1 Nephi 2:12.
2. 2 Nephi 32:6.
3. 3 Nephi 25:2.
4. Mosiah 27:30.
5. 1 Nephi 10:11.

9. SURE AS IRON

1. 1 Nephi 5:10–17; 7.
2. 1 Nephi 15:25.

10. ACCORDING TO THEIR HEARTS

1. Alma 37:36.

11. ISRAEL TO THE RESCUE

1. 1 Nephi 20:19.
2. 1 Nephi 19:24.
3. 1 Nephi 22:2–3.
4. 3 Nephi 5:25–26.

5. Omni 1:13–14, 17–19; Alma 17:18–20, 23; 53:17–20.

12. A Savior for Our Children

1. See also 2 Nephi 6:17.
2. 2 Nephi 26:7.
3. 2 Nephi 10:2.
4. Jacob 4:17–18.
5. See, for example, Jacob 5:4.
6. Jacob 6:7.
7. Alma 5:37.
8. 2 Nephi 10:22; 29:2.
9. Mosiah 27:14.
10. See also Mosiah 27:23.
11. Helaman 5:23–24, 27–30, 33–36.
12. 3 Nephi 22:13.
13. 2 Nephi 9:3.

13. Your Afflictions Will Be Gain

1. 2 Nephi 2:1.
2. 2 Nephi 2:3.
3. 2 Nephi 2:4.
4. Alma 12:26–27.
5. Alma 14:7–26.
6. Alma 10:11.
7. Alma 15:18.
8. Helaman 5:44.
9. 2 Nephi 9:18; Enos 1:27.

14. A Seer Will Be Raised Up

1. See footnote to Genesis 30:24, LDS edition of the Bible.
2. Mosiah 8:17.
3. 1 Nephi 11:17.
4. 2 Nephi 3:13, 24.
5. 2 Nephi 3:8–9.
6. 2 Nephi 3:14.
7. 2 Nephi 3:11.
8. 2 Nephi 3:21.

9. 2 Nephi 3:20.
10. 2 Nephi 3:19.
11. 2 Nephi 3:15, 23.
12. 2 Nephi 3:12.

15. Patience for Those Who Don't Know

1. Mosiah 3:16.
2. Moroni 8:8.
3. Moroni 8:16.
4. Alma 42:30.
5. Moroni 7:16.
6. Mormon 8:19.
7. Moroni 8:12.
8. Mosiah 3:20.
9. Mosiah 3:21.
10. Mosiah 8:20.

16. A Church That Can Heal

1. 1 Nephi 17:40–42; Helaman 8:11–15.
2. 3 Nephi 9:13.

17. High Interest Investment

1. Alma 34:38.
2. 3 Nephi 28:18; 4 Nephi 1:1.
3. Alma 17:2–4.
4. Alma 26:15.

18. A Book That Keeps Whispering

1. 2 Nephi 29:1.

19. The Ancients Will Not Be Forgotten

1. Mormon 5:20–21; 9:36–37.

20. The Wisdom of Angels

1. 2 Nephi 31:12.
2. 2 Nephi 28:21–22.

3. 2 Nephi 31:7.
4. 2 Nephi 31:8.
5. 2 Nephi 31:13.
6. 1 Nephi 11:6.
7. Alma 36:22.

21. YOU WILL KNOW WHAT TO DO

1. 2 Nephi 31:13.
2. 2 Nephi 32:2–3.
3. 2 Nephi 32:3.
4. Alma 37:40.

22. RICHES FOR THE RIGHT REASONS

1. Mosiah 4:26.
2. Mosiah 4:24–25.
3. 2 Nephi 4:35.
4. 1 Nephi 15:32. See also Jacob 2:19; Mosiah 4:26.
5. Alma 37:7.

23. EACH PERSON IS PRECIOUS

1. Jacob 2:21.
2. Jacob 2:21.

24. VIRTUE IS WORTH ANY COST

1. Mosiah 3:18.
2. Jacob 3:11. See also Jacob 2:28.

25. A FEAST FOR THE FIRM

1. 1 Nephi 17:17, 51–52; Jacob 7:3–15; Mosiah 17; Helaman 7:10–12; 9:16–38.
2. 3 Nephi 24:13–14.
3. 3 Nephi 12:8.

26. GROWING IN FAITH

1. Jacob 4:6.
2. Jacob 4:6; Mormon 8:24.
3. Alma 18:41–19:13.

4. Alma 19:10.
5. Alma 19:8.

28. SAVING THOSE WHO WANDER

1. Jacob 4:17–18.
2. 2 Nephi 8:21–23, 25.
3. Jacob 5:47–48.
4. Alma 32:28.
5. 2 Nephi 6:8–11.
6. Jacob 6:7.

29. SOARING AMID DARK CLOUDS

1. Alma 50:22–23. See also 1 Nephi 20:18; Alma 26:27; 31:30–31, 38.

30. THE WHOLE SOUL

1. 2 Nephi 9:42.
2. 3 Nephi 9:19–20.
3. 3 Nephi 9:13; 10:12.
4. Mosiah 5:12.

31. USING THE VERY WORDS

1. 1 Nephi 1:12.
2. Mosiah 1:2. See also 1 Nephi 4:14–15; 5:8.
3. Mosiah 1:6.
4. Mosiah 1:4.

32. IT ALL COUNTS

1. Alma 41:3.
2. Alma 41:5.
3. Alma 41:13–14; Mormon 9:14.

33. HE NOTICES IMMEDIATELY

1. Alma 35:14.
2. Alma 43:4, 6, 13, 43–44; 48:5. Compare Mormon 2:15.
3. Alma 34:31.
4. Alma 35:6–9.

5. Alma 37:46.
6. Alma 18:9–10.

34. THE DEBTS ARE PAID BY A GOD

1. Alma 34:10, 13; 2 Nephi 9:7.
2. 1 Nephi 19:12.

35. THE HEIRS ARE THE ONES WHO LISTEN

1. 2 Nephi 4:33.
2. Mosiah 15:12.

36. MODEST LEADERS HAVE POWER

1. 1 Nephi 21:2–3.
2. Alma 1:26. See also Alma 26:12.
3. 2 Nephi 8:16.
4. Mosiah 2:15.
5. Mosiah 2:11, 16–18.
6. Mosiah 2:30.
7. Ether 3:2.
8. Ether 3:5.
9. Alma 26:22.

37. HE TAKES HIS CHURCH SERIOUSLY

1. Mosiah 26:6–10.
2. Mosiah 26:13–32.
3. Mosiah 26:17.
4. Mosiah 26:18; emphasis added.
5. Mosiah 26:20; emphasis added.
6. Mosiah 26:21; emphasis added.
7. Mosiah 26:22; emphasis added.
8. Mosiah 26:22; emphasis added.
9. See also Mosiah 27:13; emphasis added.
10. Alma 5:60.
11. Mosiah 26:33–34.
12. Mosiah 26:35–36.
13. Mosiah 25:24.
14. Alma 5:57.
15. 1 Nephi 22:25.

38. LIVING PROPHETS AND NEW LIFE

1. Mosiah 5:2.
2. Alma 5:13.
3. 1 Nephi 4:20–35; 2 Nephi 1:30–31.

39. REPENTING INTO HIS ARMS

1. As well as dogs and cats.
2. Helaman 13:11.
3. Alma 15:1–12.
4. Alma 31:6–7.
5. Alma 39:2–5; 42:30–31; 43:4–5, and so on.
6. Alma 10:5.
7. Alma 5:37.
8. 2 Nephi 31:17.
9. 2 Nephi 4:35.

40. PROMISES TO THE LAMANITES

1. Enos 1:11, 16.
2. Enos 1:10–16. See also Alma 9:16–18, 24; 17:15; Helaman 15:11–13, 16; Mormon 7:1–5.
3. Helaman 15:10. See verses 7–8.
4. 3 Nephi 6:14.

41. WE WILL STAND BEFORE HIM

1. 2 Nephi 9:41.
2. Mosiah 29:12. See also Mosiah 16:1; Alma 46:39.
3. 2 Nephi 9:10, 12–13.
4. 2 Nephi 9:11, 21–22; Mormon 3:20.
5. 2 Nephi 9:4.
6. 1 Nephi 15:30.
7. 2 Nephi 9:14.
8. Enos 1:27.

43. Being Led Away from Temptation

1. Alma 34:39.
2. 3 Nephi 18:15.

44. He Loves All His Children Everywhere

1. 2 Nephi 26:33. See also 1 Nephi 1:14; Jacob 4:10; Alma 37:12.
2. Mosiah 4:7.
3. 2 Nephi 26:24–28.
4. Ether 12:33.
5. Mosiah 4:5.
6. Alma 26:16.

45. Teachers with a Familiar Voice

1. Helaman 5:30.
2. Mosiah 4:1.
3. Mosiah 23:14; Alma 11:22.
4. Alma 37:33–34.
5. Alma 5:14; 13:1–2.

46. A Hard Paved Road

1. See Alma 31:27–28; 32:1–3.
2. Alma 16:1, 9–11.
3. Alma 41:8.

47. Growing Your Tree

1. Alma 32:35.
2. Alma 32:31.

49. Prospering Is a Simple Matter

1. Jarom 1:8–9; Mosiah 1:7; 2:31, 41; Alma 1:29; 15:7–8; Ether 7:26.

50. The Ongoing Drama of the Book

1. Alma 37:2, 12.
2. Mormon 8:16.
3. Alma 37:19.

51. The Big Secret About Love

1. Mosiah 15:7–9.

52. The Vital "Space" beyond Death

1. Alma 42:4.
2. Alma 40:9.
3. 2 Nephi 2:25.

53. The Glorious Resurrection

1. Alma 7:25.
2. See Boyd K. Packer, *Teach Ye Diligently*, 274.

54. The True Faith and the True Church

1. 2 Nephi 30:6.
2. 2 Nephi 30:7.
3. Mosiah 4:8.
4. Alma 5:41.

55. Disabling the Devil

1. 1 Nephi 22:26–28; 2 Nephi 24:2–4; Ether 8:26.
2. Alma 48:20.
3. Alma 48:1, 3, 7, 11.
4. See Alma 49:5–9, 19–20.
5. Alma 60:11, 23.
6. Alma 50:1–4, 6, 12, and so on.
7. Alma 51:16.
8. Alma 48:12.
9. Alma 48:11, 13.
10. Alma 48:17.
11. Moroni 9:6.

56. The Word and Our Return Home

1. Alma 32:23.
2. Alma 31:5; 26:13.

57. THE ONE SAFE SPOT

1. 3 Nephi 14:24–25.
2. Helaman 3:21.
3. 2 Nephi 25:26; Alma 10:11; 22:18, 23; 23:6, 18.
4. Alma 56:47–48; see an example of the outcome in Alma 57:26–27.

58. HANDS THAT CAN SEAL

1. 4 Nephi 1:27, 34, 41.
2. Helaman 10:5.
3. 3 Nephi 10:7.
4. 3 Nephi 10:8.

59. THE UNFETTERED OFFERING

1. Moroni 7:8.
2. Mosiah 23:7.

60. THE GROWN-UP CHILD OF GOD

1. Mosiah 4:22.
2. Mosiah 4:20.
3. Mosiah 4:23.
4. Mosiah 4:26.

61. HEAVEN HONORS A QUIET DEVOTION

1. 3 Nephi 13:23–24.
2. Alma 5:14.
3. 3 Nephi 13:16–22.

62. THE GENEROSITY OF GOD

1. 2 Nephi 25:23; Alma 34:18, 38 ; 4 Nephi 1:11.
2. Alma 9:26.
3. Alma 34:20–27; 3 Nephi 14:9–12.

63. A SIGN OF REAL GOODNESS

1. Alma 17:28;18:5.
2. Alma 18:40–41.
3. Alma 19:30–36.
4. Such as Sunday.

64. FULFILLING THE LAW TOGETHER

1. Jacob 4:4–5.

65. HIS EYE IS ALWAYS ON ISRAEL

1. 1 Nephi 20:9–10.
2. 2 Nephi 26:15.
3. 1 Nephi 21:14, 16, 20–21; 2 Nephi 24:2; Omni 1:6–7.
4. Words of Mormon 1:4.

66. ALL MAY JOIN THE CHOSEN FAMILY

1. Omni 1:14–19; Helaman 6:10.
2. 1 Nephi 22:7.
3. 2 Nephi 6:6; 2 Nephi 10:9.
4. 1 Nephi 13:30, 32, 34.
5. 2 Nephi 26:12, 16.
6. 2 Nephi 30:1.

67. A SOLEMN TESTIMONY TO OUR FATHER

1. Alma 7:15–16.

69. INVITING, INCLUDING, AND SAVING

1. 1 Nephi 19:24.
2. Mormon 3:12.

70. IMITATING HEAVEN

1. 3 Nephi 11:28.
2. 3 Nephi 11:29–30.
3. Alma 40:12.
4. Alma 4:8–9.

71. A Steady People in the Latter Days

1. 3 Nephi 20:18–19, 21.
2. 2 Nephi 6:14, 17.
3. Alma 1:27–28.
4. Alma 1:29, 32.
5. 2 Nephi 14:5–6.
6. 2 Nephi 20:20–22.
7. 2 Nephi 23:22.
8. 2 Nephi 8:3, 11.
9. Alma 11:22–25.

72. For the Children of the Prophets

1. 3 Nephi 17:21–25.
2. Mosiah 28:7.

73. A Holy Destiny for the Jews

1. Mormon 5:20–21; 7:5, 10.
2. 2 Nephi 10:5–9.
3. 1 Nephi 19:13–14.
4. 1 Nephi 19:15. See also Mormon 3:21.
5. 1 Nephi 15:19–20; 2 Nephi 25:11.
6. 3 Nephi 20:37.
7. 3 Nephi 24:4.

74. A Marvelous Work to Do

1. Mormon 8:34; Ether 13:4–10.
2. Mosiah 13, 17, 18:1–2.
3. 3 Nephi 21:10.

75. The Dark Things Will Pass Away

1. See also 2 Nephi 24:5, 12.
2. See 3 Nephi 24:5.

76. A Greater Savior Than We Think

1. 2 Nephi 19:2.

77. True Servants, Future Kings

1. Alma 2:30.
2. Alma 17:23.
3. Alma 27:26; 28:1; and so on.
4. 3 Nephi 24:13–15.
5. Mosiah 26:20.
6. 2 Nephi 16:8.
7. Jacob 1:17–19; Jarom 1:11; Words of Mormon 1:17–18.

78. Elijah and the Hearts

1. Jacob 3:7.
2. Mosiah 5:15; 3 Nephi 20:26.
3. 1 Nephi 10:13.
4. Mosiah 2:6; 3 Nephi 17:3.

79. A Day of Greater Knowledge

1. 2 Nephi 27:7, 10–11; Ether 3:27; 4:6–8.
2. 3 Nephi 26:10.
3. 2 Nephi 27:11.
4. Mosiah 27:31.

80. Ensuring a Holy Church

1. For example: 1 Nephi 1:6; 2 Nephi 4:24; 32:9; 33:12; Enos 1:11–12; Mosiah 3:4; 10:13; 26:13–14; and so on.
2. 2 Nephi 6:11; 26:13; Alma 10:23; Mormon 5:21; and so on.
3. 3 Nephi 17:15–18; 18:16.

81. A Book That Persuades the Right People

1. 2 Nephi 26:16.
2. 1 Nephi 22:8–9.

3. 1 Nephi 5:18, 21–22.
4. 1 Nephi 22:9, 12; Ether 8:26.

82. BEING RAISED TO A GREAT GATHERING

1. Mosiah 2:41.
2. See 2 Nephi 27:33–34.
3. 2 Nephi 22:6.
4. Mosiah 18:7.
5. Mosiah 18:8.
6. Mosiah 15:23; 18:9, 13.
7. Mosiah 2:41.

83. A WORLD RESERVED FOR THE GUILTLESS

1. 1 Nephi 16:2.
2. Alma 19:13.
3. 1 Nephi 1:8.
4. 2 Nephi 8:11.
5. Alma 36:22.

84. A BOOK OF VITAL THINGS

1. Mormon 8:28.
2. 1 Nephi 13:35.
3. 1 Nephi 13:36, 40–41; 15:14.
4. 1 Nephi 15:13–19.
5. Jacob 1:4.
6. Words of Mormon 1:11.

85. TREATED LIKE ROYALTY

1. Mormon 9:10.

86. THE ONE WAY OF FREEDOM

1. Mosiah 29:11.
2. Mosiah 29:12–13.
3. 2 Nephi 1:9, 20.
4. Alma 43:45, 48–50; 53:17.
5. Mosiah 23:23.
6. Helaman 4:21.
7. Helaman 4:22.
8. Helaman 4:22.
9. Helaman 4:23.

10. Helaman 4:24.
11. Mosiah 29:19.
12. Mosiah 29:20.

87. BELIEVE AND SEE

1. Ether 4:15.
2. Ether 4:14; Alma 33:16, 20.
3. Ether 4:16.
4. 1 Nephi 11:6; Alma 19:6.

88. A MIGHTY ANCHOR

1. Ether 12:9, 11.
2. Alma 17:36.

89. THE POWER TO CHANGE

1. Ether 12:27.
2. Ether 12:26.
3. 1 Nephi 17:46.

90. THE POWER TO REJOICE

1. Mormon 8:34–37.
2. 1 Nephi 18:15–16, 20–22.
3. 1 Nephi 18:21–22.

91. POWER AS WELL AS PRIESTHOOD

1. 2 Nephi 1:24; Alma 17:9; 3 Nephi 20:41; Moroni 7:31.
2. Alma 17:11.
3. 2 Nephi 4:7, 9.

92. DISCERNMENT EQUAL TO THE BATTLE

1. Moroni 7:11.
2. 1 Nephi 19:9.
3. 2 Nephi 9:39.

93. GOODNESS LEADS TO MORE GOODNESS

1. Moroni 7:5, 11.
2. 2 Nephi 2:1–5.
3. Ether 4:12; Omni 1:25.

95. A Universal Gift

1. Moroni 7:48.
2. Moroni 7:48.

96. Launching a Wonderful and Lawful Journey

1. See Nephi's longer summary in 2 Nephi 31:13–21.

97. Perfect Rest for the Mind

1. Moroni 4:3; 5:2.
2. Moroni 9:26.

98. The Power of Confirmation

1. 1 Nephi 5:5–9.
2. Moroni 10:4.
3. 2 Nephi 9:4; Mosiah 23:27; 24:12, 16.

99. Never a Question of Power

1. Probably all of them.
2. See Moroni 10:8.
3. Moroni 10:23. See also 1 Nephi 17:30.
4. Moroni 10:8.
5. Moroni 10:18.

100. Becoming Spotless and Perfect

1. Mormon 9:6.
2. Moroni 10:33.

101. Conclusion: An Appointment with Prophets

1. Ether 5:6.
2. Moroni 10:3.
3. Alma 37:16–17; Helaman 8:15–16; 3 Nephi 27:18.
4. Mormon 8:22.
5. 2 Nephi 33:11, 13.

INDEX

A

Accountability, 32–33
Adoption, 72–73
Afflictions, 28–29
Alcoholic, 88–89
Alleys, 152–53
Ammon, 54–55
Ammonihah, 95
Anchor, 178–79
Angels, 42–43
Anger, 142–43
Apostles, 16–17
Arguments, 142–43
Athletes, 23, 70–71
Atonement, 70–71; accountability and patience and, 32–33; love of God and, 90–91; fulfilling law and, 130–31; change and, 180–81
Attitude, 128–29, 168–69

B

Backhoe, 160–61
Ball court, 70–71
Baptism, 43, 160
Basket, 120–21
Behavior, 128–29
Belief, 176–77
Birth, of Jesus Christ, 12–13
Blessing: for children of prophets, 146–47; priesthood power and, 184–85; of perfection, 202–3
Blocks, 44–45
Bodies, 108–9
Book of Mormon: promises and, 2; hope in, 3; whispers, 38–39; Lamanites and, 82–83; drama of, 102–3; as stage, 160–61; persuades right people, 164–65; as book of vital things, 170–71; rejoicing and, 182–83
Books, 122–23

C

Callings, 162–63
Car, 49, 178–79
Care center, 46
Cave, 188–89
Change: throughout life, 40–41; of heart, 78–79, 128–29, 158–59; humility and, 180–81
Charity, 190–93
Chastity, 50–51
Cheerfulness, 60–61
Children: wayward, 26–27, 58–59; Atonement and, 32–33; dream of, 41; virtue of, 50–51; acting as God's, 122–23; God loves and knows his, 132–33; of prophets, 146–47
Church, 76–77, 110–11
Church Office Building, 8–9
Church of Jesus Christ of Latter-day Saints: as marvelous work, 150–51; building, 162–63
Comfort, 198–99
Commandments, 174–75
Comparing, 48–49
Confirmation, 198–99
Contention, 142–43
Corianton, 81
Covenants, 3, 136–37

D

Dark things, 152–53
Death, 106–7
Deliverance, 4–5
Dental retainer, 138–39
Depression, 88–89
Devil, 112–13. *See also* Satan
Discernment, 186–89
Disputations, 142–43
Distribution Center, 150–51
Division, 164–65
Doll, 140–41
Drama, of Book of Mormon, 102–3
Dream, 41

E

Eagle Scout project, 44–45
Elijah, 158–59
Enemies, 72–73
Evil, 186–87
Example, 92–93

F

Faith, 42–43; building, 54–55; is like
    a seed, 96–97; true, 110–11;
    scripture study and, 114–15; comes
    in stages, 160–61; in God,
    172–73; belief and, 176–77; in
    God's gifts, 200–201
Family: Jesus Christ as foundation of,
    116–17; contention in, 142–43;
    turning hearts in, 158–59; charity
    and, 190–91
Family scripture study, 64–65
Farmer's walk, 180–81
Feast, 52–53
Firmness, 52–53
Forgetting, 136–37
Foundation, 116–17

Freedom, 174–75
Funeral, 40–41

G

Gains, 28–29
Gathering, 166–67
Generosity, 46–47, 122–23, 126–27
Gentiles, 134–35
Gifts, 120–21, 200–201
Giving up, 140–41
God: having trust in, 4–5; will prepare
    way, 6–7; love of, 90–91;
    relationship with, 98–99; acting as
    children of, 122–23; private
    relationships with, 124–25;
    generosity of, 126–27; fulfilling
    law of, 130–31; knows and loves his
    children, 132–33; is unchanging,
    172–73; freedom and, 174–75;
    rejoicing in, 182–83; priesthood
    and, 184–85; gifts of, 200–201
Goodness, 188–89
Good works, 66–67
Gratitude, 168–69
Guatemala, 38–39
Guilt, 168–69

H

Handel, George, 169
Happiness, 107
Harmony, 120–21
Hats, 126
Healing, 34–36, 172–73
Heart: turning, 22–23, 158–59;
    sacrifice and, 70–71; change of,
    78–79, 128–29, 158–59
Heaven, 142–43
Heavenly Father. *See* God
Heir, 72–73
Hiss, 38–39
Holy Ghost: receiving, 43; receiving
    guidance through, 44–45;

cheerfulness and, 60–61; Book of
Mormon and, 171; repentance and,
194–95; comfort and, 198–99
Homes, 142–43, 190–91
Hope, 3, 140–41, 178–79, 196–97
Horses, 104–5
House, 176–77
Human sacrifice, 70–71
Humility, 88–89, 94–95, 180–81,
195
Hunger, 86–87

I

Indianapolis 500, 106
Individual worth, 48–49
Inspiration, 56–57, 114–15
Iron rod, 20–21
Israel, 24–25, 132–33; Gentiles and,
134–35; establishment of,
144–45; Book of Mormon and,
170–71

J

Jesus Christ, 3; as prophet of prophets,
8–9; birth of, 12–13; life of,
14–15; judgment and, 16–17; will
manifest himself, 18–19; turning
your heart toward, 22–23; mercy of,
32–33, 154–55; healing and,
34–36; following, 42–43;
accepting kindness of, 52–53;
redeems whole soul, 62–64;
responds immediately, 68–69; as
eternal sacrifice, 70–71; robe of,
72–73; Church and, 76–77;
judgment before, 84–86; as
foundation, 116–17; fulfilling law
and, 130–31; remembering,
136–37; will bless children of
prophets, 146–47; will bless Jews,
148–49; change and, 158–59;
Book of Mormon and, 170; as

anchor, 178–79; goodness comes
from, 188–89; charity and,
190–91; can calm sorrows,
196–97; being perfect in, 202–3
Jews, 148–49
Judgment: before Apostles, 16–17;
comparing and, 48–49; before Jesus
Christ, 84–86

K

Kindness, 52–53
Kings, 156–57
Knowledge: gaining, 36–37, 96–97;
hungering for, 86–87; comes in
stages, 160–61

L

Lamanite queen, 54–55
Lamanites, 82–83
Lamoni, 54–55, 128–29, 168
Lathe, 108
Latter days, Nephi sees, 10–11
Latter-day Saints, 144–45
Law, 130–31
Leaders, 74–75
Lehi, 168–69
Library, 122–23
Life: of Jesus Christ, 14–15; causes
change, 40–41
Light, 36–37
Limhi, 4–5
Lint, 22–23
Lori, 110–11
Love, 104–5; of God, 90–91; prayer
and, 192–93

M

Manifest, 18–19
Maria, 38–39
Marni, 80

Marriage, 98–99, 104–5
Marvelous work, 150–51
Mayan culture, 70–71
Meekness, 195
Meeting, 204–5
Meltdown, 80–81
Mercy, 32–33, 98–99, 154–55
Miller, Sister, 172–73
Mission: of Jesus Christ, 14–15; prospering in, 100–101
Modest leaders, 74–75
Moroni, 2–3, 112–13
Mosiah, 174–75

N

Nan, 46
Nash Rambler, 49
Nehor, 95
Neighbors, 8–9, 120–21
Nephi: commanded to get plates, 6–7; sees latter days, 10–11; rejoices, 182–83
Nephites, 174–75, 196
Nigeria, 24–25
Nourishing, 58–59

O

Obedience: Lord's response to, 68–69; to prophets, 72–73
Odindu, 24–25
Olive tree, 26–27, 58–59
Opinions, 142–43

P

Paracelsus, 186–87
Parents, 142–43
Patience, 32–33
Peace, 142–43
Perfection, 202–3
Pigs, 86–87

Pilot, 100–101
Pink, 22–23
Plane, 100–101
Plan of Salvation, 204–5
Plates, 6–7, 20–21, 64–65
Poc-de-Poc, 70–71
Power: of modest leaders, 74–75; of priesthood, 184–85
Prayer: receiving answers to, 10–11, 126–27; for children, 40–41; for help with temptation, 88–89; to find retainer, 138–39; work and, 162–63; for house, 176–77; for charity, 192–93; repentance and, 194–95
Priesthood: sealing and, 118–19; healing power of, 172–73; power of, 184–85
Private, 124–25
Progression, 160–61
Promises: Book of Mormon and, 2; Jesus Christ keeps, 68–69; to Lamanites, 82–83
Prophets: Jesus Christ as prophet of, 8–9; judgment and, 16–17; building faith through, 54–55; obedience to, 72–73; bring about change of heart, 78–79; children of, 146–47; prayers of, 162–63; meeting, 204–5
Prosperity, 100–101
Public, 124–25

Q

Questions, 126–27

R

Racing, 106
Railroads, 132–33
Rambler, 49
Ranking, 48–49
Rejoicing, 182–83

Relationships, 98–99, 120–21, 124–25
Remembering, 136–37
Repentance, 43, 80–81, 120–21, 194–95
Representatives, 184–85
Rest, 106–7
Resurrection, 106–7, 108–9
Retainer, 138–39
Revelation: personal, 10–11; understanding, 56–57; hungering for, 86–87; scripture study and, 114–15; receiving, 126–27
Riches, 46–47
Righteousness, 86–87
Robe, 72–73
Rock, 116–17
Rod, 20–21
Roksana, 36–37
Rope, 188–89
Royalty, 172–73
Ruins, 118–19

S

Sacrament, 136–37
Sacrifice, human, 70–71
Satan, 112–13, 186–87
Savior, 154–55. *See also* Jesus Christ
Scripture study, 64–65, 114–15
Sealing, 118–19
Seed, 96–97
Seeing, 176–77
Seer, 30–31
Serpent, 34
Servants, 156–57, 184–85
Service, 46–47, 100–101
Ship, 144–45
Simplicity, 56–57
Sincerity, 88–89
Sins, 194–95
Smell, 186–87
Smith, Joseph: testimony of, 11; as seer, 30–31

Sorrow, 152–53, 196–97
Soul, 62–64
Space, 106–7
Spiritual growth, 36–37, 194–95
Stages, 160–61
Stairs, 18–19
Storm, 116–17
Strength, 180–81
Student body president, 124–25
Success, 100–101
Suffering, 196–97
Swimming team, 179

T

Teaching, 92–93
Temple, 18–19
Temptation, 88–89
Testimony: of Jesus Christ, 8–9; of Joseph Smith, 11; growing, 36–37, 96–97
Timing, 68–69
Toxicology, 186–87
Trains, 132–33
Tree, 128–29
Tree of life, 12–13
Trials: growing through, 28–29; remaining cheerful through, 60–61; humility and, 94–95
Trust, 4–5
Truth, 110–11

U

Unbelief, 176–77

V

Vasili, 36–37
Virtue, 50–51
Vital things, 170–71

W

Way, preparation of, 6–7
Wayward children, 26–27, 58–59
Weakness, 180–81
Whispering, 38–39
Whole soul, 62–64
Widow, 122–23
Will, 122–23

Women, 50–51
Word, 114–15
Work: Church as marvelous, 150–51;
    prayer and, 162–63
Worthiness, 50–51

Z

Zeezrom, 80–81
Zoramites, 68, 95